MW01488555

Drink
Smoke
Pass out

Drink
Smoke
Pass out

An unlikely spiritual journey

JUDITH LUCY

VIKING
an imprint of
PENGUIN BOOKS

VIKING

Published by the Penguin Group
Penguin Group (Australia)
707 Collins Street, Melbourne, Victoria 3008, Australia
(a division of Pearson Australia Group Pty Ltd)
Penguin Group (USA) Inc.
375 Hudson Street, New York, New York 10014, USA
Penguin Group (Canada)
90 Eglinton Avenue East, Suite 700, Toronto, Canada ON M4P 2Y3
(a division of Pearson Penguin Canada Inc.)
Penguin Books Ltd
80 Strand, London WC2R 0RL England
Penguin Ireland
25 St Stephen's Green, Dublin 2, Ireland
(a division of Penguin Books Ltd)
Penguin Books India Pvt Ltd
11 Community Centre, Panchsheel Park, New Delhi – 110 017, India
Penguin Group (NZ)
67 Apollo Drive, Rosedale, North Shore 0632, New Zealand
(a division of Pearson New Zealand Ltd)
Penguin Books (South Africa) (Pty) Ltd
Rosebank Office Park, Block D, 181 Jan Smuts Avenue, Parktown North, Johannesburg, 2196, South Africa
Penguin (Beijing) Ltd
7F, Tower B, Jiaming Center, 27 East Third Ring Road North, Chaoyang District, Beijing 100020, China

Penguin Books Ltd, Registered Offices: 80 Strand, London WC2R 0RL, England

First published by Penguin Group (Australia), 2012

10 9 8 7 6 5 4 3 2 1

Text copyright © Judith Lucy 2012

The moral right of the author has been asserted

All rights reserved. Without limiting the rights under copyright reserved above, no part of this publication may be reproduced, stored in or introduced into a retrieval system, or transmitted, in any form or by any means (electronic, mechanical, photocopying, recording or otherwise), without the prior written permission of both the copyright owner and the above publisher of this book.

Cover Design by John Canty © Penguin Group (Australia)
Text Design by Adam Laszczuk © Penguin Group (Australia)
Typeset in 11.5/18 pt Sabon
Printed and bound in Australia by McPherson's Printing Group, Maryborough, Victoria

National Library of Australia
Cataloguing-in-Publication data:

Lucy, Judith.
Drink, smoke, pass out : an unlikely spiritual journey / Judith Lucy.
ISBN 9780670074914 (pbk.)
Lucy, Judith.
Women comedians–Australia–Biography.
Spiritual biography–Australia.

792.7028092

penguin.com.au

For Mrs Wagon

CONTENTS

INTRODUCTION

Some of you may be a little familiar with the book *Eat, Pray, Love*. It's a woman's search 'for everything' after a horrible divorce. The author's search takes her to Italy, India and Bali. Coincidentally, the last three countries I've been to are the same ones, and in the same order, although there were returns home in between. In Italy, Elizabeth Gilbert ate what she liked and lost weight, and had to swear to be celibate for a year because she'd always had men in her life; in India, she did yoga, stayed in an ashram and had some sort of spiritual breakthrough; and in Bali, she looked for balance in her life, met an incredible healer and wound up banging a hot Brazilian whom she went on to marry. I have nothing against this writer and I know that many women have loved this book. However, I couldn't have less in common with Elizabeth Gilbert if I was just a gas.

I've had several years where I've been celibate; the difference is that I was often desperately trying to have sex. If I had eaten everything I wanted to in Italy, I would have come back the size of a small zeppelin, and as it was I was constipated and sleeping in a room with my seventy-year-old birth mother, and the only man who came onto me was so short and so wide, he was virtually a circle.

I went to India on a spiritual journey too – in fact, for the TV show I made for the ABC, *Judith Lucy's Spiritual Journey*. While my ten days there was a great experience, the only yoga I did was on the roof of a boat, which nearly landed me in a neck brace. It was taught to me by a man who was so incompetent and bored that I may as well have just had diarrhoea for an extra day, because I could have had a more enlightening experience in a toilet.

And after finishing the show, I went to Bali. I didn't meet my future husband, and the 'healer' I encountered massaged my breasts. That wasn't the first time this has happened, either – my jugs must seem so tense.

I guess what I do have in common with Elizabeth is our desire to make shitloads of cash by telling our stories. Gee, that's not what I meant to type, let's try that again: What we do have in common is the fact that we were both pretty depressed and wanted to work out why and how to live a better or more fulfilling life.

My 'journey' didn't take place over a year, but for the past forty-four. I grew up a staunch Catholic, but when I turned my back on that religion I believed in nothing and threw myself into my career, good times and finding Mr Right, believing that one or all of the above would make me happy. Not that I had any idea what being happy really was, but gradually I started to realise that none of these things seemed to be working, and when my parents died within ten months of each other, it made me start to question everything, even though I don't think I was aware of that for some time.

While I was slowly recognising that booze, boys and comedy might not hold the answer to the meaning of life, I was also developing a real love of yoga (try not to feel nauseous), which led me to an interest in spirituality (a word I still struggle with). At some point, I realised that I was less anxious, less desperate for a drink and not quite so dependent on circumstances dictating my state of mind. I was less of a pain in the arse. I really did feel better and I thought it might be worth writing that down. And though the idea for the book came before the idea for *Judith Lucy's Spiritual Journey* (and actually before I read *Eat, Pray, Love*), I've written about the experience of the television series as well.

I'm not living in a cave in the Himalayas, I'm single and I still drink (sometimes I still drink a lot). But I *am* less fucked up, and I thought, why not share a story that's sort of about spirituality, but doesn't take itself too seriously, and has no eating, less praying and loving, and a lot more drinking, smoking and passing out, because if my tale didn't have those elements, it would just be a pamphlet.

1

SOLI DEO GLORIA
(Glory Be to God!)

I'm adopted. My birth mother, Jan, came from a Catholic family so, when asked, her preference was that I too be raised in that faith. I recently had the conversation with her where I said, 'But didn't you see the awful irony that you were condemning me to the same religion that made you think you'd sinned by having sex outside of marriage?' I'd like to report that this was a decision she had agonised over, but her reply was: 'I didn't really give it much thought.' (Thankfully, also her approach to contraception.)

So, as I suspect has often been the case, a decision that has defined me was probably made while dunking a Butternut Snap into a cup of tea.

A couple of years ago I was having a very pleasant lunch with a friend and her mother, who happened to be a 'spiritual adviser'. Regrettably, that didn't mean she was someone you called if you were in a jam while making a tequila sunrise. She helped people fill their 'God-shaped hole'. Elizabeth was a lovely person (who has now gone to her God) and I found what she did genuinely fascinating, until she said, 'Oh, so you were brought up Catholic? You know, you all go back to it in the end.' I wanted to scream, 'ARE YOU OUT OF YOUR MIND? I'M MORE LIKELY TO DIG UP AND FELLATE ONE OF THE THREE STOOGES!' Mercifully, I refrained from offering my thoughtful rebuttal to this kind and gentle woman, but it was painfully clear that she had hit a nerve.

For those of you who aren't Catholic, and especially if you were brought up without any kind of religion, try to imagine that from pretty much the moment you were born you were told a preposterous story as though it was completely true. Imagine you were told that there is a mystical roll of pressed chicken that can speak Mandarin. It can also travel through time, heal all sexually transmitted diseases and recite every episode of *Joanie loves Chachi*. Not only did your parents tell you this, but you went to some building once a week with a whole bunch of other people who believed it also, and you continued to worship the pressed chicken at school with the other kids for twelve years. It might have been over a decade before you encountered anyone who said, 'Hang on a minute, I reckon that's baloney.' It might have been years before you realised that millions of other people follow a type of flamenco guitar–playing terrine, or a kabana sausage that writes poetry, or don't believe in any type of deli good at all.

Our family, Tony and Ann Lucy and my older brother Niall, were Catholics, and for years it was all I knew. My parents were Irish, so I guess Catholicism was as much a given for them as Guinness, leprechauns and not bathing (actually, that could have been just my family). My grandmother had holy water in her house and jigged in the kitchen. Mum loved the rosary and telling us how much she wanted to kill English people (no contradiction there). Religion just seemed to come with the Val Doonican records. And I suspect that was the case for many of their generation: you were born into a religion and you accepted it, because that's what your parents had done.

So it was as normal for us as . . . well, come to think of it, not that much about our family was normal,* so why not believe in some chick being turned into a pillar of salt or some chatty shrub on fire? Although, having said that, my father was fairly ambivalent up until the end when, like many lapsed Catholics, he seemed to want to have a bet each way. And my brother got out as soon as he could (or maybe it was just that his flares made it impossible for him to kneel anymore). So maybe it was really only Mum who was sincerely committed to Catholicism.

While we went through all the motions that our faith dictated, there was never the slightest idea that this religion brought anyone the tiniest bit of joy. Mass was openly viewed

---

* See *The Lucy Family Alphabet* to find out what our family's idea of normal was (and because I could really do with the royalties).

as an unpleasant chore (ideally, our family would have attended a drive-through service, preferably one with fries), my Catholic school fees were 'exorbitant', and even Mum seemed to find serving up fish fingers on a Friday during Lent a massive pain in the arse. But while it seemed to be barely tolerated, it was never questioned. It was like our family had a collective case of herpes – it was a drag and no-one was happy about it, but there was really nothing that could be done.

Mum openly prayed but no-one talked about the wonder of God or universal love, or what they believed at all. There were no spirited discussions about the doctrine, and not even the slightest interest in getting to know the people in our local parish, even though we went to church there for years and I went to school with most of the children. We went to the football and we went to mass. The Lucy family followed the Claremont Football Club and were Roman Catholics, end of discussion. And we were a helluva lot more excited about a premiership than life everlasting.

I know some people raised in the Catholic faith who from a very young age thought that it was all nonsense, but this simply never occurred to me – though nothing ever did. I was the least curious, most accepting child alive. I just did what I was told and tried to do it well, because I was a suckhole. At school, I was determined to be as 'good' at religion as I was at turning a piece of felt and an egg carton into a wonderful mother's day gift. (It's a jewellery box!)

From a very early age I prayed like a motherfucker. Mum prayed about everything, so I guess I took my cue from her. I had all the equipment: rosary beads, a large statue of Mary and even the beginnings of self-loathing. The first two were presents – I mean, who wants KerPlunk? – but the last, I was born with. Adam and Eve screwed up in the Garden of Eden, so you're guilty even before you've stolen your first Cherry Ripe (not that I would have dreamed of doing such a thing).

I loved Mary, in particular, I think because she was a woman. I prayed to her constantly. God freaked me out. I couldn't understand 'eternity' or the idea that he (and God was very much a He) was *everywhere*. This is the sort of concept that as an eight-year-old you consider when you're on the toilet. Even then I remember thinking that it was more than a little bit creepy, and that surely the Big Guy had better things to do than watch me on the can. But Mary was one of us. My parents argued a lot, so I was always asking for the Virgin to make that stop, without a great deal of success. It never entered my head that getting no result meant that I should stop asking and hoping. Sure, I was an imbecile. But I think this was one of the reasons Catholicism really got its hooks into me. I thought I could do something about a situation where I was, in fact, completely powerless.

I was constantly on the lookout for miracles. Once, I was convinced that I had seen the eyes blink on my plastic statue of Jesus. The truth was I had been staring at it for so long that it's surprising I didn't see it start breakdancing. The idea of faith was an obsession. I loved that line from the Bible: 'If you have faith as big as a mustard seed you can move a mountain.' I had faith as big as a giant hot dog, so I'd stand in our garden and literally will mounds of dirt to move. In Grade One, I roped my best friend into trying to bring dead leaves back to life. We used a lot of matchboxes and wet tissues, rather than the power of prayer, but we believed – if God could bring a person back from the dead, why couldn't we revive a frond or two? Or, at least, *I* believed. After a while, my buddy obviously thought I was a weirdo and ran off with a girl who was more keen on playing kisschasey than hanging out with rotting foliage. With the wisdom of hindsight, I think she made the right call.

My little experiments might have seemed weird even to others at my Catholic school, but to me they fitted in with the mystical, almost magical, stuff going on around me. While still in primary school, I had my First Communion and was also Confirmed. I know the latter sounds like something that should involve a restaurant reservation, but it is, in fact, when you receive the Holy Spirit. I have no idea how we were meant to 'receive' it, or if it involved an orifice. Or even what it was. And these were in the days when it was called the Holy *Ghost*. This stuff made *Nanny and the Professor* look like a documentary. I remember not having the slightest idea what was going on, but the Catholic Church doesn't much mind that – most people are baptised (and hence connected to God FOR ALL ETERNITY) when the only thing they're interested in is their mother's rack.

(Years ago, a friend of mine refused to christen her child, only to find her mother-in-law slyly trying to re-create the ceremony with water she pretty much got out of a toilet.) I don't think Limbo exists anymore, but the idea was that if a child wasn't christened and then died, it would spend all of eternity hanging out with the other dead babies, unable to get into heaven. Now, isn't that a religion that just screams FUN?

Nor did I have a clue what was happening with the First Communion. This light-hearted ceremony is when you first receive the tasteless bit of wafer thought of as Christ's body, called the Eucharist. The fact that eight-year-old children are involved in some sort of spiritual cannibalism is strange enough, but before you can chow down on the holy bread you must go to Confession, where you have to tell a priest all your sins and receive forgiveness. And, of course, the priest wasn't just some guy in a weird muu-muu, he was representing GOD Himself. It turned out that, for a child, more stressful than owning up to your many sins was coming up with something to say, which meant, at times, you'd make stuff up. I admitted to running a brothel.

My only really concrete memory of the First Communion ceremony – other than the general, grudging participation of our family – is of my brother and Aunt Paddy being my sponsors. They were also my godparents, because the Lucy family wasn't exactly social. It was either ask them or try and pass off a couple of blow-up dolls, *Lars and the Real Girl*–style.

I also remember being dressed like a seventies bride for both Confirmation and First Communion. One of my classmates wore a denim pinafore to her Holy Communion, which my mother loudly expressed was so sacrilegious that she may as well have been wearing nothing but an anklet. Mum was never really big on the whole 'love one another as I have loved you' thing. She was a practising Catholic who always needed a lot more practice.

The other major scandal from this period of my childhood was that when I was in Grade Four, our teacher – Sister Dorothy – left the convent. We knew something extraordinary had happened the day she turned up in normal clothes telling us to call her (I think it was) Miss Price. Actually, she still sort of dressed like a nun. I guess if you've worn a habit for years, it becomes a, well . . . In any case, you're not going to suddenly turn up looking like Lady Gaga (much as I would have liked to have seen her in stilts and a fish head). Before we found out why she became a non-nun she just disappeared. Not in a hostage-situation way. I just don't think she taught at the school anymore – although, as no-one ever mentioned her again, the former remains a possibility. She was gone. It was just something else to be confused about.

By high school, I think a lot of girls viewed religion as a great class to sleep through. I was still enthusiastic but mystified. My best friend Michelle and I attended a 'stranger camp'. Although it sounds like a get-together of lolly-bag-clutching paedophiles, it was billed as a gathering of male and female Catholic students who wanted to explore their faith. More like a gathering of male and female Catholic students who wanted to explore each other's genitals. At least, that's what Michelle and I had hoped, but it was no hot bed of hanky-panky, just the scene of a lot of earnest role-playing games. In any case, it turned out the kind of boys who attend this sort of thing are a good deal more socially retarded and physically repulsive than the girls. (Although I do remember one of the male youth workers giving us teenage girls a lot of massages – he was no idiot.)

The earnestness wound up being fine with me, since the reality was that I was as relaxed around boys as I was around red-back spiders and would have been less alarmed to have one of the latter in my pants. I embraced it all with such sincerity that on the final night I broke down and accused my fellow students of not taking the camp seriously. I was seventeen. Someone should have just tied me down, poured Bundaberg Rum down my throat and told me to go out and get fingered instead of obsessing about living Christ's teachings.

My lasting recollection is that we all had to write a letter to ourselves, about our faith, which we would receive after we'd left school in exactly a year's time. I can't remember what I wrote, but it turns out that it should have been: 'Dear Judith, You now think this is all a bunch of horseshit. Under no circumstances tell any of your university friends that you took part, and wandered around the countryside, clutching a candle while singing, "This little light of mine, I'm going to let it shine".'

Oh my God, I really did do that.

I prayed regularly and genuinely all the way through school. I said all the right things and like almost every Catholic girl I've ever met, for a while I wanted to become a nun. Yet there was something I just wasn't buying. As I got older, I started asking more and more questions in religion class. I treated it like a physics problem, certain that with the right information I could solve this metaphysical equation. But I never seemed to get the right answers. In retrospect, my doubts had been piling up for some time.

By and large, I wasn't brought up to believe that God was a fearful and vengeful old man who could damn me to an eternity of wailing and gnashing of teeth. We were told that 'hell' was simply being away from God's presence. Apparently, once we had seen His face we would never want to be away from it – who knew God looked like Viggo Mortensen?

Ours was the generation that grew up on the *Good News for Modern Man* Bible. What a ridiculous title. How hard was the Church trying to be 'groovy'? I don't know why they didn't call it *Great Shit for Funky Brothers and Sisters* and be done with it. The *Good News* Bible was a relatively recent translation of the New Testament, and was accompanied by drawings meant to look cool and minimalist but that just gave the impression the artist couldn't be bothered giving anyone an actual face. The point was to show us that Jesus was a cool dude who was all about the love, man. (Although, I'm confident I'm not the only one who was irked by the parable of The Prodigal Son. There are two sons on a farm. One of them does all the right things and follows his father's wishes, while the other one pisses off and spends his money on booze and hookers, kind of like a modern-day sportsman. But when the bad boy returns to the farm, penniless, his father is so happy to see him that he makes a huge fuss and kills his best cow, leaving the other son to be fairly put out. The father tells the good son off and everyone cries, 'Hooray, Shane Warne is back!' Now where is the justice in that tale, I ask you?)

It was pretty smart of the church to downplay the Old Testament, which makes the *Saw* movies look like *Annie Get Your Gun*. For instance, God asks Abraham to kill his only son Isaac as a sacrifice to Him, but it turns out that the Big Guy is only testing Abe and He stops His follower at the last possible second. Now that's what I call a tribal challenge! People think *Survivor*'s gruelling? I'd like to see one of those tanned gym bunnies part the sea or deal with a plague of frogs. (I truly would.) But the Lord had the doozy of all reality programs happening years ago. Unfortunately, it was called *God's Just a Little Bit of a Cunt*.

Looking back, though, I think my disillusionment with Catholicism was triggered not by the texts but by my mother.

She was the most devout adult I knew but there was simply no getting around the fact she was completely miserable. No doubt this was more to do with my father's indifference than the Heavenly One's, but even so, her dedication seemed to bring her little comfort. (Or so I thought for a long time.)

And while there was certainly a sense of the mysterious about what we were taught at school, I don't remember ever feeling a sense of celebration or wonder despite, at one point, being taught religion by a good-looking young man who would play us catchy hymns on his guitar and who, fantastically, was called Mr Fox. (Looking back, maybe we just thought he was good-looking because most of the other male teachers wore terrible shorts and wouldn't have looked out of place in *Planet of the Apes*.)

Then there were the Mercy nuns, who rarely displayed that quality. Fortunately, only a handful of them taught, and while a couple of them were lovely, some of them seemed genuinely demented and/or insane, and were certainly terrifying. While Sister Florence, the primary school headmistress, was reprimanding us one day, I became so overwrought that I started smiling. She reacted as though she'd caught me fucking a goat, which involved screaming at me and, I think, threatening disembowelment. My brother once told me the story of how one of his classmates had had a similar nervous reaction to a very angry Christian Brother. When asked why he was smiling, the young boy, who I'm guessing was thrashed on the spot, replied, 'Just happy.'

These doubts were in the back of my mind. The first time I remember consciously thinking that the teachings didn't make entire sense was as a twelve-year-old, when we were informed that masturbation is a sin. This made no sense to me. How could doing something with your own body, which hurt no-one, be wrong? Especially when it felt that good and was free? If the Catholic Church thinks that God doesn't let you into heaven for that one, I can only assume that it's just him and a couple of armless people behind the Pearly Gates. And that's not even true, where there's a will there's a way – I once saw a pre-pubescent girl have the time of her life using nothing but the corner of a couch, much to the mortification of her parents.

When I was sixteen, another nail was hammered into the coffin of my faith by a book about feminism that a girlfriend of my brother's lent me. I don't remember much about the book other than it was a revelation. It confirmed my increasing suspicion, after a priest had told me that a woman couldn't have an abortion under any circumstances, not even if she'd been brutally raped, that this religion I'd been brought up with was not exactly 'lady friendly'.

And the smaller injustices were mounting up. A friend of mine was expelled just before we graduated from school for cheating – something she'd clearly done because of the huge pressure to do well – and she was left to sit her final exams without any academic support, amongst strangers. It seemed unlikely that while grappling with this decision our high school headmistress,

Sister Sheila, had asked herself the question: 'What would Jesus do?' As she looked out over the incredible views from our beautiful school grounds, she may well have reflected on the real gift of the Catholic Church – procuring prime real estate.

So by my last year of high school (during the obligatory Sartre phase), all of this was starting to add up. I still prayed like a dying priest for good exam results, but I was a lot less interested in the contents of the Bible reading I gave at our graduation mass than in my performance of it – my university course in theatre arts was just months away, where I would become the kind of wanker that really should have been considered sinful.

In the end, I didn't walk away from the Church; I just lost interest in it. It was one of the things that I wanted to shrug off along with school, my parents and youth. And on some level, I probably felt like I had given it my best shot and it still just didn't make much sense to me.

Only after I started studying Marx at university did my drift away from Catholicism become open revolt. The whole 'religion, opiate, people' thing made me feel that I'd been the victim of a terrible hoax for the last eighteen years of my life. No wonder my questions about belief in God never got a straight answer in religion classes – it was all a lie! Religion was just an elaborate story to oppress the working class . . . semiotics is the study of everything that can be taken as a sign . . . male hegemony . . .

paradigm . . . Literature 111 . . . did someone say 'free keg'?

And religion didn't do much good. Dad had a massive heart attack a couple of months after I started university. It was terrible for all of us and Mum was just distraught. We went to the cathedral across the road from the hospital every night after visiting him, but by then I felt it was a complete waste of energy and that our time would have been better spent making it home in time to watch *Sale of the Century*. Instead of Mary, I may as well have been praying to Delvene Delaney for all those years.

The fact Dad lived had nothing to do with God's intervention, and as soon as he was well enough to come home, I announced that it was the end of the road for me and the Pope. My parents put up very little argument, probably because they were exhausted, so that was that. I didn't feel guilty about the decision, just angry. I wanted to get on with my life as an adult as far away from all this Catholic mumbo jumbo as possible.

Apart from saying she prayed for me, once I'd left the Church and her home, my mother never mentioned religion around me. Dad had never talked about it much anyway. I spoke more about it with friends who were fellow lapsed Catholics, like when an old buddy Andrea and I saw a film called *Priest*, and we both admitted to reciting the mass despite ourselves, word for word, along with the actors. Andrea had no hope – she was brought up in a house with a 3D crucified Jesus on the wall, whose eyes followed you around the room.

Andrea was one of my few new university friends who'd

even been brought up Catholic, so it really didn't come up. I do remember a bunch of theatre students going to midnight mass at the end of my first year of study. My buddies thought it was hilarious and, standing up the back of the church, made fun of the proceedings. Despite the fact I'd rejected the whole ridiculous ball of wax, I felt so uncomfortable that I had to walk out. I wouldn't set foot inside a church again for many years.

I might have been able to walk out of a building but Catholicism has always been my Hotel California – I've checked out, but . . . I'll never completely know how it's affected me. I can't erase the first eighteen years of my life. Catholicism is the background that defines everything else. Last year, my birth mother, Jan, and I went on a holiday to Italy. If there's one thing you're going to do in that magnificent country it's look at churches. I was astonished to find that after all these years it greatly bothered me when I saw fellow tourists happily photographing the interiors of these beautiful buildings with complete disregard for anyone who might be actually praying. It was like I had turned into Jesus and wanted to banish the merchants from the temple. I am equally outraged if I hear about someone receiving Holy Communion during a Catholic mass if they're not Catholic, or if a lapsed one receives it without having gone to Confession. Obviously, I feel fine about priests sodomising children, but you have to draw the line somewhere.

And I really do enjoy talking about it all with fellow survivors. There are a lot of us out there. I didn't feel like I was in a club when I grew up with Catholicism, because for so long I didn't realise that there were any alternatives. But I feel like I'm in one now. It's like a lot of things – if you didn't experience it, then you don't really get it, and I have to admit that it's fun to roll your eyes about it with people who understand. That is, of course, those of us who were lucky enough not to experience the religion's darker side.

I was so busy running away from my upbringing, or maybe more accurately, trying to throw myself into my future, that I never stopped to wonder if there was anything about Catholicism I missed. But I think there was. It was more than a sentimental attachment to churches. A close friend, who wasn't brought up with any religion, has always maintained that those of us who were always find themselves attracted to the spiritual side of things. I don't know if that's necessarily true, but maybe I did miss the comfort and hope that prayer could sometimes provide, along with the idea that there was more to life than our immediate existence.

The irony is that I thought that I left the Church because I wanted something 'real', something concrete. And yet I didn't realise how concrete what it had offered me had been: you live a good life, you follow the rules, you believe in God, you die and go to heaven. Not only did that provide a template for day-to-day living, but it also answered the questions of why we were here and what was going to happen when we died.

Jesus, now what was I going to do?

2

COMEDY

If anything has defined me over the years, it's been my job. Not my children, my marriage, my beauty, my money, my birthmark, my sex life, my prosthetic leg, my cocaine addiction, my car collection, my love of travel, my harmonica playing or my pet Chihuahua Jade Hurley – mainly because most of these don't exist. In the last twenty-three years, family members have died, friends have come and gone, my engagement ended and I've moved houses and cities, but I have remained a stand-up comedian.

I'll be honest – I don't really understand people who don't work. My mother wasn't allowed to and I think it was one of her greatest frustrations. I understand that some women are happy being full-time homemakers, but she wasn't one of them, and maybe it's because of her that I always felt a career was very important.

Work has often been the thing that has kept me sane and given me any sense of responsibility that I have. It was where

I derived almost ALL my self-worth. When other aspects of my life were turning into a shit sandwich, I would always comfort myself with the thought that at least my career was under control. If work was going well, then, I believed, so was I.

I worked very hard when I was at school. I was no genius; I was just smarter than an egg timer and had nothing else to focus on, so completely devoted myself to study. I mistakenly believed that the odd elephant stamp might grab my parents' attention. In fact, results made no difference to Mum and Dad, who would only have noticed my marks if I'd dug Karl up. My parents weren't very demonstrative, they were just wrapped up in themselves and each other. Dad's time was taken up with working and drinking. Mum's time was taken up with dieting and obsessing about Dad. And both of them were flat out screaming at each other to 'drop dead' and applying large amounts of makeup. (That's right: Dad wore makeup.)

I look back on those years and wish that I'd spent them smoking, drinking and kissing boys (I wound up discovering these joys about seven years after everyone else). I really mean that: no-one tells you that you won't ever use a protractor again, but you'll never forget that first kiss. I really thought the most important part of my life was getting good grades. Positive results brought momentary delight and mistakes brought days of self-inflicted torture. Wisely, I turned this approach to making a living and decided, from a very young age, that I wanted to be a performer. (Just to clarify my idiocy, I was busting a gut to get top marks not to study medicine, but to do a BA. I could have spent high school shelving Rohypnol and I probably still would have gotten in.)

I threw myself into whatever I was doing. My first job was at a gourmet deli called Pretzel Pantry, and I put such concentration into slicing up fancy cheeses that you would've thought I was performing a circumcision. Whether I was cleaning toilets in a restaurant or making sandwiches in a vegetarian café, I wanted to excel.

This was apparently lost on my supervisor, Mrs Kanters, when I was working in the napery section of a large department store at age sixteen. Mrs Kanters had a perfectly dyed, blonde, pudding-bowl haircut and wore so much bright blue eye shadow that it looked like she was trying to re-create the sky. I'm afraid her body also reflected her name, in that she was a little reminiscent of Phar Lap. She didn't take a shine to me and seemed unaware of the love and dedication that I poured into her section of tea towels and tablecloths. I worked with a girl who wouldn't have known a placemat from a crack vial but she had old Seabiscuit fooled. The one and only time I was late for work and was caught by Mrs Hey-why-the-long-face, I knew that the writing was on the wall. The following week she took me into the storeroom and told me that I was not 'cut out' for napery. I cried like I'd just seen a favourite pet being clubbed to death with a horseshoe.

I'd clearly attached way too much importance to my job,

but it was also pretty obvious I was desperate to please and to be liked by everyone. I guess that made my career choice fairly clear-cut.

I don't know what planted the acting seed, but apart from the short-lived nun phase, I can't remember ever wanting to do anything else. A lot of my friends took a few years to work out what they wanted to do and a couple still don't know. While I often think that what I've wound up doing is kind of insane, I feel lucky that I always knew I wanted to be a performer of some description. I've often questioned it (at times daily), but weirdly, it's always given me some kind of grounding.

I was one of those unbearable kids who fantasised about their Academy Award speech. When I tired of that, I'd pretend I was a guest on a chat show when I was on the toilet. (I had no idea how appropriate that was, considering the crap that can come out of my mouth when I give interviews these days.) Essentially, I wanted Meryl Streep's career: critical acclaim, respect, wonderful parts and bone-crushing fame. I assumed that when I wasn't filming or preparing for another complex, Oscar-winning role, I would be posing for *Vanity Fair* or blowing Warren Beatty (that desire might have come a little later in life). I wanted it all. I wanted to be one of those stars snapped without their makeup, or revealed to have dimply thighs or a baby bump on the cover of every trashy tabloid. I really assumed that international adulation would make me blissfully happy. FOR THE LOVE OF GOD, WHY DIDN'T MY

PARENTS PAY ME MORE ATTENTION?

I don't want to make a gross generalisation about all performers, but a lot of us are just a yawning chasm of insecurity and self-obsession. I have no doubt there are some postal workers who are like this too, but my guess is that they keep it to themselves or just snap one day and shoot a bunch of people. For most of us, there is simply not enough affirmation in the world.

I think the appeal of performing is twofold: you want the acclaim and love after your brilliant performance, but also, while you're doing it, it's a great form of escape. Although I know a lot of really interesting people who buried themselves in books when they were growing up, I wasn't one of them. I bathed myself in everything from *Gilligan's Island* to *Another World* to *Man About the House*. As a kid, my way of avoiding life was watching television. I really do remember wanting to be inside the box and I must have finally worked out that the way to do this was to become an actor. When I wasn't watching *Get Smart*, I was pretending to be Agent 99, and at some point I must have thought, 'What? People actually get paid to do this shit? This is a JOB?'

As I grew older, I lost my taste for magazine covers and TV and fell more in love with the actual craft of acting. I wanted to make a living as a well-respected stage actor. I remember performing a monologue from *Joan of Arc* in high school and just disappearing: I was completely in the moment, time was immaterial and I had absolutely no sense of 'me'. What a relief. I think I was able to really 'become' Joan because a classmate had once tried to set me on fire with a Bunsen burner.

I did as much acting as I could at school, but at university, blissfully studying theatre arts, I THREW myself into performing. Who doesn't love university? I was surrounded by likeminded people (today, some of my closest friends are from this time), I was studying something I loved and there was a tavern. I was involved in something like seventeen productions in two years. I literally worshipped at the church of student theatre. I had to take some other units but my life revolved around the theatre department. There was nothing I didn't love about it. I loved rehearsing, I loved doing the actual plays and I loved the cast parties. I wish I'd gotten laid, but that's my only complaint.

With the notable exception of Olivia (not her real name), a person who would go on to play a big part in my life, all my other socialising was with my fellow acting students – and were we wankers! There seemed to be a party every weekend and everything was an excuse to perform. There was one game we played that involved pretending to be whatever the winner of the last round suggested: so, someone would say something like, 'Now everyone has to be Bert from *Sesame Street* discovering Ernie in bed with Patrick Swayze, while stoned.' You get the idea, it was just an excuse for everyone to be HILARIOUS.

Strangely, not everyone thought we were as funny as we did.

I was in a production where three of us had to dress in black from head to foot, including shapeless black hoods where even the hole for our eyes was covered in black mesh. We looked like demented apiarists. We thought it would be fun, during a rehearsal break, to go to the local chicken take-away shop in costume. The fifteen-year-old girl serving us would have been subjected to this sort of student behaviour regularly, I'm guessing, and didn't bat an eyelid. As we were leaving, I turned to her and said, 'Beware of the bees.' Nothing.

We did the embarrassing trust exercises, the vocal warm-ups and the dreadful productions. Some of them weren't dreadful but inexperience blighted most shows. I was cast in a tremendous play as a woman who had an affair with one of her husband's colleagues. Unfortunately, the one thing we hadn't rehearsed was the two of us kissing in makeup. This meant that on opening night my husband walked into the living room to find me chatting casually to a man with so much lipstick smeared over his face that the dialogue really should have involved him saying, 'Oh this? No, I just like rubbing my face with raw beetroot.'

I took it all very seriously. I was cast as the lead in a play called *The Greatest Woman in the World*, the Maria Montessori story. It was a big deal because one of Perth's best-known local actors was directing and it was produced on the university's main stage, as opposed to the little upstairs one that was used for student-directed pieces. All this meant that people other than your parents might actually see it.

One of the scenes involved Maria vomiting and almost faint-
ing when she was studying medicine and witnessed her first
autopsy. It goes without saying that I was a method actor, so
I took myself off to hang out with some cut-up cadavers in the
medical department. The experience nearly turned me into a
vegetarian but was essentially a complete waste of time. I really
did try to use it to re-create Maria's horror and nausea during
the scene, but pretty much just made noises like a cat with a fur
ball and swooned a bit like Miss Prissy in a Foghorn Leghorn
cartoon. Apparently, you couldn't just snap your fingers and
'become' someone else summoning up any experience at will –
well, I certainly couldn't.

I was all too aware of simply being Judith Lucy the night the
lighting technician deliberately kept the lights up for a very long
time at the end of the first act as a practical joke. Word had gotten around that my leading man had shocking halitosis and the
first half of the play concluded with he and I kissing as the stage
went to blackout. Why couldn't I have experienced feeling that
ill during the operating scene?

Regardless of bad breath, the constant need for positive
feedback and the lows of a bad show, I remember those couple
of years incredibly fondly. I ignored any misgivings I had, especially when it came to my own talent.

Before completing my degree, I moved from Perth to
Melbourne, where I knew only one person, to hopefully study
acting full time. While I now know that I was also fleeing my

family, I viewed everything as just treading water until I could attend a proper drama school in Melbourne and devote myself to being an actor. I gave up my buddies and all security to pursue the one thing that I thought gave my life meaning. I had no idea that I would abandon the idea so easily once I had arrived in my new home.

My plan was to do as much acting as I could before the auditions for the Victorian College of the Arts came up some eight or nine months after my arrival. I was living in a share house, far from home, and I was giddy with freedom, tempering my acting ambitions with a newfound love of alcohol and good times. Still, I found work doing front-of-house for a well-respected theatre and volunteered for various performance-based festivals.

I also scored the lead in a VCA students' production of *Fire and Ice* (the story of Mary Shelley). I was convinced this would mean I would be a shoo-in by the time the acting auditions had come around, as the teachers would already have experienced my blinding talent. It wasn't quite the experience I'd hoped for. We rehearsed at the drama school, which, unbelievably, was nothing like the movie *Fame*. I was also disillusioned by the fact that the staff didn't seem supportive of the director at all (hence very few of them witnessed my genius), and lastly, I had to kiss a man who smelt like a piece of parmesan cheese.

Who needed a boyfriend? I was pashing men whose various odours really made me swoon. My acting experiences weren't all about sucking face, though – there was at least one play where I *didn't* have to make out. Thanks to my front-of-house job I appeared in a production that was generally described as a junkie soap opera, called *In Angel Gear*. I had actually started doing comedy by that stage, which is why I was the light relief. Mercifully, that meant that I was also one of the few people who didn't have to take their clothes off. When I tell you that before each performance the entire cast had to dance, one by one, with the director, looking into his eyes, to Sinead O'Connor's 'Nothing Compares to You', you'll hopefully understand why that whole experience made me want to take my own life.

I was also seeing a lot of theatre when I first moved to Melbourne, though the majority of it was, to say the least, far from inspiring. Years later, I was walking down a mall in Adelaide at four in the morning during the fringe festival and passed a crowd of people watching a council worker dig a hole. I think they were drunk and had confused it with a show. Well, the labourer's work was a masterpiece compared to some of the shit I'd sat through, and I may have been in a Beckett play that was not too dissimilar.

Slowly, my doubts about a life in the theatre were starting to pile up. But not my doubts about the stage – I still loved everything that went with it, including being on it. The problem with acting had always been that you relied on others for work. I hated the idea of waiting for the phone to ring. I was also starting to realise how dependent the profession is on physical appearance, and that the most talented person didn't always get the job. And that I was not one of the most talented people, anyway.

Thankfully, I'd always had a plan B. One of the other reasons I'd wanted to come to Melbourne was because I knew it was the comedy capital of the nation. Even at university, though I didn't like to admit it to myself, I'd started to wonder if I was only just competent when it came to acting. I had, however, thought for some time that I might be . . . funny. At both school and university, whenever we were given a drama assignment to devise ourselves, I generally played it for comedy. I've always enjoyed making people laugh. My father was funny, as is my brother, and a sense of humour was vital at school – thanks to weird parents and generally being a goody-two-shoes, without it I would have been the smelly, friendless girl in the corner. And there really is nothing like making someone – anyone, a small group or a classroom – laugh, to fill you with the notion that 'they like me, they really like me!' I mean unless you make suits out of human skin, who doesn't want to feel that? I may have been just a little more desperate.

So gradually, I lost my desire to become a serious actor and slowly became more and more interested in the world of comedy. I'd never gone to any live stand-up in Perth, but I'd seen a little of it on television and was obsessed with both the D-Generation and *Australia You're Standing In It*. I had no idea what to expect when I went to the comedy theatre restaurant The Last Laugh – and it blew me away. Everything about it seemed magical to me: the wacky décor, the even wackier waiters (ironically, they were almost all studying drama at VCA) and, of course, the shows. There were straight stand-ups but there was also cabaret, and groups that specialised in song parodies or slapstick; there were sketches, jugglers, funny magicians and a woman who played the saw. I'd died and gone to heaven. And these people had clearly written their own material (well, most of them), and were creating their own work. That appealed to me immensely. While comedy had been my back-up plan, it had been a pretty nebulous one. But now that I was witnessing it, I started to believe it was something that I might actually be able to do. And there was nothing pretentious about comedy. People were there for a good time and I was starting to be all about good times.

And so, the night before my VCA audition, I did something I was starting to excel at – drank a skinful. I would have smelt, and certainly performed, like a plum pudding. I didn't care. Besides, a lot of people got into acting through comedy. Instead of berating myself for poor preparation and irresponsible behaviour, I took my failure as a sign and a confirmation all in one: I was *meant* to pursue stand-up comedy. I was Mary Tyler Moore. After I walked out of the audition room, I wanted to throw a hat in the air – I was going to 'make it after all!' I was probably still drunk, so it's a miracle I was able to make it across the street.

And wouldn't you know it? Thanks to stand-up I *have* ended

up acting in a couple of movies. These experiences, where I've been around proper actors, have only confirmed for me that I never would have won that Academy Award I thought about on the toilet. Maybe I would have improved, but I think I was always a little too self-conscious. Really great actors do seem to be able to lose themselves in a character and take risks with the role (sometimes too many risks, such as Nicolas Cage in . . . well, most things – he appears to be in several different movies at once in *Bad Lieutenant*, and I'm afraid none of them are good). But I don't think I was ever quite brave enough to do the thing that had appealed to me about acting in the first place – let go of being me. So I turned that on its head by being me on stage, as a stand-up comedian. And at least with stand-up you don't have to wait for the reviews. You know immediately if you've failed.

I made my first attempt at stand-up a year after moving to Melbourne and didn't have the slightest idea what I was doing. I don't just mean on stage. I was twenty-one and I could barely dress myself. I hadn't even worked out that I really needed to start wearing a bra and I had NO IDEA about men. I certainly hadn't lost my virginity. The only males I'd kissed were a priest, guys on stage and my best friend's brother. What a pity I didn't turn that into a routine, instead of appearing on stage one night wearing nothing but a green garbage bag and pointy rubber ears. I really thought props were the way to go when I started. My first attempt involved water pistols, wrapping the audience in toilet paper and pretending a kabana sausage was a rattlesnake.

For a long time, I was awful and I came close to giving it up on countless occasions, but I was always lured back by my complete lack of other options and – having experienced a career that might involve partying and staying up late – my strong desire not to have a normal nine-to-five job. Actually, if they were the only criteria, maybe I should have become a prostitute.

I wonder what would have happened if someone had pulled me aside and said, 'You're a really anxious person and stand-up is about as relaxing as having breast implants made out of nitro-glycerine. I should also mention that you have a tendency for alcohol abuse and you will almost exclusively perform in venues with a bar, at night, on your own. Apart from that, it seems like a really sound decision. Unless it's too late to talk you into being a suicide bomber.'

Of course, the other handy thing about it was that these terrible early gigs confirmed my fairly low opinion of myself, which made the idea of plugging away and trying to figure it out even more irresistible, because that would clearly fix everything. Even though I may have believed that, and desperately wanted to be a part of the comedy world, the magic of The Last Laugh certainly wore off once I started actually performing there. It was where I did my first-ever gig and I worked at the famous theatre restaurant for several years, off and on. I did have some great times, but quickly learnt that a comedy audience is not necessarily where you will see people at their best, especially at a midnight show. A friend of mine once remarked that stand-up was the only Dickensian form of entertainment left, and the fact that one night a human turd was allegedly found under a table at this historic venue would seem to back that up. It was often full of bucks' and hen's nights crowds, who are generally not there because they're connoisseurs of fine humour.

One night, a bunch of men mistakenly wound up at an all-female night of comedy, thinking that might involve – who the hell knows? – a nude pillow fight? They asked the staff if anyone knew of a live sex show they could attend afterwards. Another time, I had the joy of telling an audience that the men would have to use the downstairs toilets, as five people had projectile-vomited in the upstairs ones. (I don't know how the staff knew it was five – maybe they'd signed their names.)

I did loads of horrible gigs when I started. My material was stretched to the limit at twenty minutes. I once resorted to getting the audience to sing TV jingles (at a venue that was burnt to the ground the following week), and another time got them to tell me the jokes. I supported a well-known American comic, dying every night along with another female Australian. One evening, a guy came up and told us how great he thought we were. I discovered later, when he abused me on my way through the car park, that he'd been acting on a dare. 'Fuck off' was my witty retort. At another gig in Moe, the only time there was laughter when I was on stage was when a man yelled out, 'Show us your whizzer!' I didn't even really know what that meant, but I was confident it wasn't a reference to sherbet. The gig ended with the entire room chanting, 'Bring back the juggler, bring back the juggler!' We had to stay the night and there was nowhere to drink but the place where we'd just performed, so I buried my head in a cocktail and was relieved when a gentleman came up and just made general chitchat. Unfortunately, about fifteen minutes into the conversation he said, 'You know, out of the three acts tonight, I reckon you were the worst.'

I think even a tub of pig fat might have started to think, 'Is this job really for me?' At one point I vowed that a gig at The Last Laugh would be my last ever shot at it, and I'd only do it because I desperately needed the eighty-seven dollars fifty. People laughed. So here I am.

Looking back, I'm amazed that I persisted. Often I would tell myself that doing horrible gigs would toughen me up. WHAT FOR? Was I going to start doing a vaudeville act in maximum-security prisons?

You certainly needed to be resilient, both on stage and off. I met some very supportive people when I began, both men and women, but I also spent many a night being the only female in a room full of male comics who wouldn't even speak to me.

I'm not entirely sure why that was. Maybe it was as simple as feeling that I was on their turf. Stand-up is still dominated by men, but back then it was virtually a monopoly, and I take my hat off to the trailblazing women like Wendy Harmer and Rachel Berger. I know I copped less crap because they came before me and copped more. I can't even tell you how furious it makes me that articles are still being written today about whether women are funny or not. (Actually, it's true I once heard a woman try and tell a knock-knock joke. 'Knock knock.' 'Who's there?' '. . . I can't remember because I have a vagina.') People are going to think what they think and you're generally better off just shutting up, working hard and selling tickets. I've been asked so many times what it's like to be a female in comedy that it just makes me want to make some jam and have a baby.

This will shock you, but I took the early lack of support from some men very personally until, one day, I had my palm read by a crazy lady at the Paddington Markets in Sydney. I think she was Russian, her nails were painted with liquid paper and she was dressed a little like a psychotic Marie Antoinette. She may also have been wearing a shower cap. What the hell, the readings were ten bucks. She gave me the best career advice of my life: she told me she had no idea what I did for a living, but that whatever it was, it was a job and only that. I should stop trying to be friends with my colleagues and just run my own race. She also told me that I had the most incredible aura that she had ever seen and that I was going to be tremendously famous, wealthy and happy and live for a very long time. I loved this fruitcake. Unfortunately, I then encouraged my two friends to talk to her.

I remember saying, 'Look, she's crazy, but I'm telling you that for ten bucks she's going to make you feel fantastic.' She told my first friend that he was mentally challenged ('I'm sorry but you are short in the mind'), and the other that she would have one son but that he would be a heroin addict who would steal everything from her ('Yes, even the curtains'). And that if she 'ever slept in the foetal position or ate baked beans again' she would die. One out of three; I still took her advice to heart.

Comedy, especially stand-up, is something that I will have a love/hate relationship with until the day I die. I'm not one of those comedians who are obsessed with comedy. I really don't know much about its history or early pioneers; in fact, I probably have a much greater knowledge of Nazi Germany (similar ground, obviously). I've never watched a Buster Keaton film. When I started, I was a huge fan of Steve Martin's stand-up, and I think the work of many local and international comics is brilliant, but I've never really studied the craft of comedy. Of course, I've been influenced by people, but I think one of the essential ingredients of being a stand-up is finding your own voice; working out what you want to say and how you want to say it. I think it took me a number of years before I achieved this (and what a shame the voice I discovered was so damned irritating . . .). It finally came together in a show called 'King of the Road', which was about, among other things, a disastrous trip overseas. It was the first time that I'd told fairly personal stories about my life, and that's when I realised I could turn awful or embarrassing incidents into cash! I've never looked back.

But comedy is not really my idea of a fun night out. While I'll certainly go out of my way to see friends perform, it's extremely rare for me to think, 'I've got a free night, I must see some comedy.' I'm much more likely to think, 'I've got a free night, I must learn to tango/make a soufflé/work on that idea about Shakespeare-performing weevils.' I love laughing, and I love making people laugh, but I think of comedy as work.

And that work can be hard (not that we're saving lives, or even doing something as useful as unblocking a sink). Stand-up, whether your material is personal or not, is a very exposing thing to do. If people don't like your act it's hard not to think that they don't like you, although I generally tried to leave this idea behind me when I walked off stage. I'd berate myself if I thought I'd made mistakes, but sometimes it's just beyond your control if, say, an audience is just too drunk, or you're following an act that is very different from your own. And then there are the reviews, which can also be a little personal. I once had one that described me as looking like 'Michelle Pfeiffer's younger sister' – happy with that – 'if a tree had fallen on top of her'.

You often spend a lot of time on your own, dealing with nerves, certainly in my case. And unlike music or theatre, *everyone* knows about comedy. Everyone has watched it, or is funny, or at least thinks they're funny, so people seldom hold back when it comes to their opinion of you and your act.

Corporate gigs can be particularly soul-destroying. They're

well paid but you're often the closing act at a conference where a group of workers just want to talk to each other and get pissed (and fair enough too). Unlike when you're performing your own show, people haven't voluntarily come to see you and you have no control over how the night will be put together. I recently entertained a group of insurance workers where I was put on after a trio of fire-juggling skateboarders and before hypnotist Martin St James. It didn't go well. The worst is when you're making a 'surprise' appearance. The last time that happened to me, the majority of the (I think they were) stockbrokers had guessed that the surprise guest was going to be . . . Delta Goodrem! Instead: 'Hi everyone, funny lady Judith Lucy here.' That also didn't go well. Although, I don't know that it went as badly as the night I performed for a bunch of accountants at some weird resort just outside of Adelaide. Moments before I went on stage, the woman who'd organised the evening turned to me and said, 'Actually the guys didn't want you, they wanted Max Walker.' It was another one of those gigs where I had to stay the night and drink with the people who'd just made it quite clear that my repertoire really needed to be something else (in this case, cricket anecdotes). When a man thirty years my senior said that he had a beach house nearby and asked if I'd rather go there and spend the night with him, it really did seem like the best option.

Of course, I've been heckled many times ('Are you a lesbian?', 'You're ugly!'), and in my experience ladies tend to get comments that pertain more to their physical appearance and inability to get a man than their jokes, which makes about as much sense as someone yelling 'You're not funny!' at Miranda Kerr when she's on the catwalk. I've had a roomful of women who worked for a weight loss company tell me that I'm fat, I've had a bunch of Australian soldiers turn on me, with one threatening to drop his pants, and I've had an ex-footballer go on the radio the day after seeing me to say that my act was so bad he wanted to take me out the back and punch me. I've even had a 'friend' say to me, after discussing the pathological hatred an acquaintance of his had for a pretty innocuous female television presenter, 'Wow, imagine how many hundreds of people must really despise *you*.' So why do it? Because I've been lucky enough to earn a healthy living out of it, and because some nights, and you never know when or why or how it will happen, everything clicks, everything just falls into place and you feel like you can't put a foot wrong. Something happens between you and the audience and it's like you're all on a wonderful date that goes so well we should really all wind up getting laid. There are no distractions, you're not thinking about what you're going to eat after the show, or which in-house movie you might watch, you're not trying to bring yourself back to the material, or wondering why the guy in the third row hasn't laughed all night. You are just completely absorbed in what you're doing; every syllable is perfectly timed, every adlib works. And it's not just about you, it's really about you and the audience – sure, you're telling the jokes, but they're giving you the thing that spurs you on. Paradoxically, you feel completely in control and not in control at all. And you really do 'have to be there'. You can't re-create that moment ever again. It's a kind of alchemy. The audience bring as much to the table as you do and the combination sometimes means that you all walk away feeling like you were part of something a little bigger than just you. That's why I love talking to the audience (when they want to be talked to), because when it's good it really is like a great conversation. (I remember once doing a routine about a certain movie. It was going well – the crowd was involved – and suddenly a man in the front row could no longer help himself. He stood up and said, 'Oh, a friend of mine worked on that film and I've got a great story!' And he did! I'd tell you what it was, but apparently I might be sued.)

My friends have grown very tired of me saying that I will NEVER do a one-woman show again and then turning around a couple of years later and acting like those words simply didn't come out of my mouth. Like a mother, I really do forget the contractions, and that touring can feel like someone has ripped you a new arsehole. I always go back to stand-up, because it's like an itch that nothing else can scratch.

Still, even when it's all going well, I'm not one of those people who only truly 'comes alive' on stage. I saw a documentary on Joan Rivers in which she said she was at her happiest when she was doing her job, and I know other comics who live for that hour or so under the spotlight. I would shoot myself in the face if I felt like that. No matter how much fun I'm having, there's always a sense of relief when it's over, and that's because, even on the best nights, you can still blow it. It really is like a date: sure, you were on fire until the entrée came, but somewhere between the braised beef cheek and the strawberry parfait, he started checking his phone messages . . . should I not have talked about my psoriasis? I once heard Jerry Seinfeld say that you can never completely relax on stage – a joke might get a huge laugh, but you can't enjoy it because you have to move on immediately and hope that the next one does too. It's like one big daisy-petal plucking game of 'they love me' that could so easily become 'they love me not'.

I'd been doing stand-up for about four years when I moved to Sydney. I moved for a couple of reasons and one of them was that my career had plateaued in Melbourne. As it happened, after a couple of months, I was offered a job on the D-Generation's *The Late Show*, which was, as they say, my big break. I'd already done pretty much everything I could to blow it, a couple of years before. Jane Kennedy had seen me perform and invited me to come in and meet the team, with the idea that I might get a weekly spot on their very successful breakfast radio program. I'm sure the meeting was arranged for a more than civilised time, like ten in the morning. Thanks to a big night,

I slept through it. A bit after ten the phone rang repeatedly. When I finally picked it up, it was Jane asking me what was wrong, why had I not made it into the station? Barely awake, I slurred into the receiver, 'Oh yeah, I slept in, whatever . . .' and pretty much hung up on her. Five minutes later, I sat bolt upright, realising that I may as well have added 'And hey, go fuck yourself.' The phone call I made then was one of the most nauseatingly apologetic and sycophantic of my life. Thankfully, she must have sensed my desperation and sincerity because they gave me another chance. I just hope to God that none of them ever do need a kidney.

The radio spot eventually led to the television show. This was the year that I learnt about 'the serious business' of comedy. While I certainly wasn't lazy, there was something about performing in bars and the fact that a number of comedians were often stoned on stage that gave the impression that trying to make people laugh was all just a bit of fun. It wasn't until I worked with the D-Gen that I realised that if you were actually concerned about making quality comedy, you had to work really hard and possibly not kick the day off with a bong. It also made me understand just how precise an artform comedy is, that a joke could be ruined if it was filmed the wrong way or edited poorly. I was generally terrified but extremely grateful for the opportunity and the huge learning curve.

It turned out my childhood fantasy that any kind of fame would put me in a permanent state of bliss was a little off the mark. The program had a pretty healthy cult following – although the paparazzi were not following my every move, so mercifully my affair with Alec Baldwin never became public knowledge – and for the first time in my life I was occasionally being recognised by strangers. Here it all was: interviews, *queue jumping*, people writing me letters (sure, not always good ones – nobody likes to be told that they have 'a body like a sack full of hammers'). It's lovely when someone approaches you because they like what you do. (Although, again, sometimes less so. There was the man who came up to me in the street and stood so close I remember thinking, 'Golly, have I slept with you and just forgotten?' He then screamed at me that women aren't funny, but that I was as funny as a man. Insulting my entire sex took a slight shine off the compliment, but we did wind up dating for a while.) But if you're already a self-conscious person, being stared at doesn't help your paranoia. I had no idea whether it was because they liked me or hated me, or because I had bird shit in my hair. I'm not complaining (well, not much), but it was the first glimpse I got of the idea that sometimes what you think will make you happy can fall short of expectation. (I'd also thought, as a teenager, that meeting Adam Ant would make me happy, but when I did meet him on a chat show recently . . . it was a bit like seeing your parents in bathers. Just a little sad.)

Yeah, poor me. It's not like I was cleaning chimneys. The thing that slice of fame *did* fix was my career. A year on a successful television program meant that I could make a living touring one-woman shows. So in my late twenties I began performing in theatres rather than in pubs, which meant that my audience was less likely to drink to the point of vomiting through their noses, and the TV exposure ensured that the majority of people who came to see me knew something of my work, and hence were less inclined to request to see my breasts. This was a big improvement, and touring has continued to be the backbone of what I do.

As is probably clear by now, I had absolutely no clue about 'building' my 'career'. I always wanted to do my best but I never had it mapped out. I never desperately wanted my own TV show or to make a movie – I didn't really know what I wanted. I mean, I pray to God that I've improved. I think I've become better at writing jokes, listening to an audience and just being more in command on stage, but Christ, after twenty-three years you'd hope so, wouldn't you? I worked hard and I always wanted to get better, but, a little like I've done everything else in my life, I just stumbled along and hoped that something would drop out of the sky.

And I was incredibly lucky. Some pretty great things did drop out of the sky. Thanks to Mick Molloy and Tony Martin, I was involved in a couple of movies, *Crackerjack* and *Bad Eggs*. They were simply two of the most fun things that I've ever done. I was very nervous about the acting side of it (although I was really just playing myself in both), but I was working with great people, I had virtually no responsibility for the final product, and I got to drink with Bill Hunter – does it really get any better than that? Yes, it does. In an eighties flashback scene in *Bad Eggs*, Mick and I, looking a little like Limahl and Pat Benatar, make out and he grabs my arse. I'm so sorry my parents didn't live to see it: they would have been so proud.

Yet, despite some professional highlights, everything about my life remained pretty haphazard. Looking back, I can't quite believe that I thought a successful career was the answer, especially when my job was so ludicrous. It would take me years to work this out, despite the advice from a ten-buck psychic.

3

BOOZE

I love drinking. For a long time, even my fantasy of heaven involved fine wine – no clouds or angels, just top company and top-shelf piss. As soon as I could, I started drinking decent alcohol, although there were certainly occasions in my early twenties when it was any port in a storm (or sherry, or muscat). I once hoed into a four-litre cask of Stanley Leasingham Moselle that had been sitting on top of the fridge for months (it was the only booze left over from a house-warming). Thanks to the heat from the ancient fridge motor, the wine seemed to have fortified, or so I thought at 3 a.m., when I announced that it was 'just delicious'. When I tried it the next day, I realised I would have gotten a tastier drop by squeezing out a cat's bladder.

But that was pretty rare. Red wine is my poison and I love the smell, the colour and the taste. I loved (and miss) the popping of the cork and still love the sound of it sloshing into a glass and, obviously, I love getting pissed. For years, nothing would make me happier than reaching the point in the day or night when

I could start drinking until I pretty much passed out. My idea of almost complete bliss was waking up after a huge night and having a lunchtime drink before the inevitable hangover set in. Not only do you get to dodge feeling lousy for a day, but you're really just topping up from the night before, so for the first hour or two it's a particularly pleasant form of inebriation. Needless to say, the following day the hangover is so awful that it's like you're a bunch of finger nails scratching yourself across a blackboard, and the paranoia has you believing that Mossad has a contract out on you. I can see how people turn into alcoholics simply because they want to avoid this feeling.

I've always scoffed at those who call themselves social drinkers. (It used to be such a popular thing to write in personal ads. I once put an ad on the internet that said: 'I hate walks along the beach, I smoke and drink and the only other thing I enjoy doing is watching TV. I have large breasts.' The response was strangely very disappointing.) But actually, the social side is one of the things I love most about booze. I've certainly gotten drunk on my own, but I LOVE getting drunk with buddies.

Initially, alcohol seemed to go hand in hand with the freedom and fun I associated with being an adult away from Mum and Dad. My father had certainly made his mark; he drank and my mother didn't – guess who looked like they were having more fun? My parents were pretty typical of their generation and nationality, I think. Dad was the big-drinking, charming Irishman and Mum was the teetotalling martyr. Dad laughed a lot more.

I believe I had my first drink at my Grade One teacher's wedding. I was the flower girl. I would've been nine and was given half a centimetre of champagne. My mother loved telling the story that when the waiter came round to top everyone up, I nodded and wanted more. I never had the heart to tell her that I'd meant to shake my head but was just shy and nervous and honestly forgot how my neck worked for a minute. And maybe it's not really such a cute story anyway, when you consider that I went on to have (well, some people might claim) *a bit of an issue*.

I couldn't have been a bigger goody-good at school, so I wasn't much interested in drinking. My older brother would buy my best friend Michelle and me half a bottle of wine to take to whatever fancy restaurant we had decided on for dinner. At sixteen and seventeen, that was our idea of a good time, pretending to be in some sort of Evelyn Waugh novel, as opposed to lying to our parents, clubbing and drinking until we puked or fell over. I was actually a little appalled when I saw my peers exhibit this kind of lack of control, not realising that a few years later I would make their attempts look Amish.

When Michelle and I both landed major parts in the school play at sixteen, we celebrated by having a couple of champagnes with her mother. I woke up the next day with a terrible cold: I was tired, nauseous and had an upset stomach. I couldn't work out how I'd caught it – what I had caught, of course, was my first hangover. Several years later, I had a similar but less endearing experience, when I drank until I lost consciousness in my living room. When I woke up I couldn't explain the bizarre wound on my hand that was weeping and painful. The chemist asked if I'd been mowing the lawn because she believed I may have encountered a poisonous caterpillar. What I'd encountered was falling asleep in front of the fucking bar heater and burning myself to the extent that I still have a scar. The first few houses I lived in in Melbourne were freezing and I regularly passed out in front of all sorts of providers of heat, which were left blazing all night. It's actually incredible that I still have hair or a face.

At university in Perth, I drank a little more, but I was still pretty uptight so I'd get tipsy and leave it at that. And I declined the marijuana that was popular with my friends because I didn't smoke and drugs were illegal. I had a couple of unfortunate experiences on tequila (one may have involved me waking up in my own vomit and my mother calling me 'an animal'), but some part of me couldn't really let my hair down until I left my hometown.

Melbourne is where I really grew up and it's also where I discovered booze. After a couple of false starts, I moved into a share house with the only person I knew in Victoria, Olivia, a girl I'd met in a film tutorial at university in WA, primarily because we both had a crush on our tutor. He wasn't the greatest teacher in the world, but I would've been happy spending the rest of my life with just one of his spectacular arms.

Olivia loved drinking. I came to love both Olivia and

drinking. And I mean LOVE. Olivia remains the funniest person that I've ever met and drinking with her was the most fun that I'd ever had. And for at least the first few years, I think that's pretty much what I got from this lifestyle – FUN. My childhood was not some kind of waking nightmare but generally when I'm asked what my favourite memory of it is, I tend to say that it was turning eighteen (i.e., when it ended). And I felt entirely free of childhood when I moved to Melbourne.

Whether you discover drugs and alcohol in your teens or early twenties, there are just so many reasons to embrace one or both: it's what your friends are doing, you're experimenting and wanting to piss off your parents, you're freaking out at becoming an adult and, frankly, it's just really enjoyable and seems to solve problems like shyness and anxiety and makes you feel a little magic (at least until the next day). That was absolutely its appeal for me. I had no idea you could just flick a switch and turn these things off. It was a complete transformation: I went from being a super-conscientious student, devoted to acting, who drank a little and never touched drugs, to someone who was well on their way to becoming a homeless person. I know most people drink a lot in their twenties, but I don't think many people – and I include hardened criminals and pirates here – drank more than we did.

Olivia had discovered drinking at a pretty early age and I couldn't have picked a better companion to show me the ropes. As well as being hilarious, she was very smart, sophisticated (certainly to my green Perth eyes), stylish and had money. She was equally at home drinking in a front bar or spending hundreds of dollars on champagne in an expensive restaurant. She had time on her hands and approached life as though it was an endless adventure. And I really did fall in love – I couldn't get enough of being around her. It wasn't a sexual thing, although one night we did suck face after five bottles of wine. I think it confirmed our heterosexuality, especially for Olivia, who claimed that thinking about it was what made her throw up so violently the next day.

Olivia was on a family allowance so she didn't have to work and I made a living as a sandwich hand. My memory (well, what little memory I have of that time) is that, if we hadn't managed to go out for lunch because I'd had to work, come nightfall we would throw back some beers, smoke any dope we had, drink a four-litre cask between us and then GET INTO OLIVIA'S CAR and go to the all-night bottle shop. On one of these many occasions, we backed into a taxi. Olivia was very good at thinking (well, lying) on her feet, and immediately accused the other driver of being at fault. I went with a different strategy and actually said, 'Oh, I'm sorry, we're just really pissed.' Thankfully, he must've had his own problems because instead of reporting us, he just sped off, seemingly grateful to get away from these two pissheads – who knows if it was even a taxi? It could have been an ambulance or a flying saucer.

To give you some indication of our lifestyle, I'll recount the events, as clearly as I can, of the night we moved in together. Late afternoon, having shifted most of the furniture, we sat on Olivia's mattress and drank three or four bottles of wine before deciding that we should go to the party that I'd been invited to by one of my co-workers at the vegetarian café, where I did my fine sandwich work. (I remember only one vegetarian ever working there, and the boss actually got his lunch from KFC – he knew what was in that tofu casserole.)

As usual, Olivia drove and, surprisingly, we were the first guests to arrive, so our very generous host plied us with champagne. At the height of the party, an American girl who worked at the café produced a tiny joint. She'd been telling us for weeks about this 'Maui Wowie' pot that was going to blow us all away, but I don't think we'd believed her, mainly because she was pretty unbearable. I remember taking one, maybe two puffs and that's really where the evening ends for me. The host of the party, Duncan, was thinking of leaving the café so, apparently, I turned to my colleague, Jeremy, once I'd passed the dope along, and asked if he would be interested in taking over from Duncan. Jeremy replied that he would. I listened to Jeremy's response and then asked him the same question six more times, before Olivia suggested that we leave and I stood up and walked into a wall.

We got into the car and, to this day, neither of us knows what happened, but presumably we had some sort of argument, because I got out and wandered the streets for hours trying to find my new home. Miraculously, Olivia, who drove around looking for me, arrived back at the same time; we let ourselves in and passed out. It wasn't until the next day that we realised our house was literally around the corner from the site of the party. Happy housewarming!

I have a lot of stories. That's what our lives were – a big series of stories. We were either telling one of our past tales or creating another one. There was the time that Olivia and I went to Hayman Island. It was a 6 a.m. flight so, as we were naturally hung-over, we kicked the day off with several bloody marys. I have very little memory of that flight but I do know that we both fell asleep and that, once we'd landed, our removal involved security guards and wheelchairs. This was another occasion where I decided to apologise, while Olivia called the pilot a motherfucker, to his face. I think this was also the trip where Olivia begged one of the hotel cleaners to have sex . . . with me. I've never been back to Hayman Island.

Things really came to a head, drinking-wise, when Liv and I moved into a share house with my old best friend from high school, Michelle. Michelle and Olivia didn't really click. Mainly because Michelle belonged to a young communist group called Resistance, who honestly believed that there was going to be a revolution in Australia (it seemed to me this was unlikely to be caused by Resistance, as there were 450 members NATIONWIDE and they seemed to spend a lot of their time plotting the downfall of capitalism while sucking on bongs). We often had members staying with us. They ate our food, drank our wine and apparently one of them actually took a banana from our fruit bowl and masturbated with it. Because of the underlying tension, Olivia and I took things up a notch. Liv was regularly found unconscious in the bath. I'd assumed that this was just the combination of warmth and alcohol but maybe they were failed suicide attempts after listening to another stoned seventeen-year-old called Lachlan wax lyrical about Lenin and the inevitability of Communist Australia. Actually, that kind of makes me want to run a bath even now.

A certain level of drinking brings on paranoia. We received very odd mail that would sometimes involve newsletters with tips on money laundering, and strange men often knocked on the door while they left their cars running. The ceiling access hole in the bathroom mysteriously lost its cover. One night, while alone in the house, Olivia heard someone cough and the lights turned themselves on and off while she was on the phone. And on another occasion, I hung up after a call and yelled up to Olivia, 'What colour is our telephone?' Perplexed, she replied that it was green. 'Not anymore, it's cream.'

We could never work out what the house had been used for before we moved in, but whether any of these activities had a rational explanation was beyond us. We had many theories, though. I was pretty confident that the seven dwarves were living in the roof.

None of this made me question my behaviour. Mainly, I think, because that would have involved remaining sober and

I was certainly not interested in that. My entire approach to life was that we were here 'for a good time not a long time', and I was mostly having a pretty good time. Although, even I realised that my life was starting to spin a little out of control in that house. I was a couple of years into my career as a stand-up comedian at this point and I'd started cancelling gigs at the last moment because of hangovers, or simply because I wanted to keep drinking with Liv. My agent told me I was starting to get a reputation for being unreliable and somewhere in my pickled brain this really bothered me.

At twenty-four, I knew that I needed a major change – and to get away from my drinking partner for a while – so when our trio disbanded, I moved to Sydney to continue my stand-up career. That was when I was offered *The Late Show*, which helped me get my act together, at least when it came to work.

You can imagine that the world of stand-up comedy, though, presented its own problems. Why do we never truly appreciate what our bodies are capable of in our twenties? When touring my one-woman shows, I really could get trashed every night, sleep most of the day, get up, perform and do it all again. I was on stage by myself, but thanks to the nature of stand-up, not alone in the bar. This may shock you, but I'm not the only comedian who has ever overindulged.

Many years ago, a journalist (that might be stretching it – she wore more makeup than a flight attendant) asked me what my beauty regime was – not a common question for those in my profession. My response: 'Well, like most comedians, I retain my healthy glow by drinking, smoking and taking drugs.' While there are exceptions, I think it's fair to say that most comics are fond of a tipple, at the very least. And because it can be a fairly solitary career, it can be a lot of fun to get together with other stand-ups, swap stories and just get off your face.

During one Hobart Comedy Festival, the drinking wasn't confined to the evening hours. The good people of Tasmania weren't interested in seeing the funny folk from the mainland and (one theory was) happily stayed at home to watch a four-part Beatles' documentary. Obviously, there was only one thing to do. I actually wound up with two comedians living on my floor, Marty and Greg, essentially because I had room service and their accommodation didn't. We kicked off every day with several bloody marys and ended every night with bottles of French champagne. (I can't quite explain how I thought that I could live like Donald Trump during this period. I dare say some people may have saved some of the money they made from touring, but all I have to show for it is broken capillaries.)

One night, a member of staff told us that we had drunk them out of Moët but that they had some lovely bottles of Australian sparkling wine. I believe I said (and I'm not proud), 'I'd rather drink my own piss.' Thankfully, we got around the problem by drinking the Australian product with shots of vodka in it.

How the hotel workers loved us! We didn't let housekeeping in and later heard that they had never seen a room left in such disgusting condition (take that, Black Sabbath). The gentlemen also thought it would be hilarious to refer to the poor waiting staff, who had to navigate my bedroom floor like an obstacle course, as 'monkey boys'. It's only just occurred to me that every room service snack we ordered must have contained some bodily fluids.

I know what you're thinking, though: 'Hang on, they drank morning and night, but what about the middle of the day?' I've always been a lover of the long lunch and there are some lovely and very scenic restaurants in Hobart. My tolerance to alcohol was obviously very high at this point, I knew the show (that no-one was coming to see) like the back of my hand, and I also knew the point at which to stop imbibing so that my performance wouldn't be affected. There was one afternoon, however, where that judgment failed to kick in.

Regrettably, the show opened with a tap dance, and while I tended to stumble through it when completely sober, I'm confident that this particular night I may have concussed several people in the front row. I don't actually think I dropped a line of the script. (It's incredible what practised drinkers can get away with if they know something well. I once saw a gifted, but very inebriated musician sing and play piano like an angel, yet between songs his banter was about as comprehensible as a budgerigar having a go at Chaucer.) I believe that the audience might have had some sort of sense that something was up, though, as I felt the need to tell them 'I'm just so pissed' every five minutes. I did occasionally add, 'I think that I'm channelling Oliver Reed.'

I'm pleased to say that that's only ever happened once. While I may have gone through an unfortunate stage of cancelling gigs, I never performed drunk again, because the guilt about letting down a group of people who'd actually paid to see my show would have killed me. Thank you, Catholicism, for possibly being the only thing that stood between me and a daily morning cocktail.

Greg and I shared a number of experiences like this and we didn't just confine them to our own shores. Once, in London, we stayed up smoking and drinking in my room until the wee hours and when I briefly left the hotel the following day I failed to lock my door properly. On my return, I was welcomed by the manager and another staff member who asked me if any of my belongings had been stolen because they were convinced that a break-in was responsible for the state of my accommodation. Later that day, I found Greg playing with a toddler in the hotel bar. It was some time before he turned to the child's parents and said, 'I'm sorry, I forgot he wasn't mine.'

That same trip I also passed out on the pavement and a black cab drove over my hair – and no, I was not wearing my Lady Godiva wig. This may be the place to talk a little bit about denial. I genuinely saw this as nothing but a funny story. A very good friend of mine once turned to me, in his late forties, and said, 'You know, I've just realised that some of my problems might have something to do with my parents.' A garden gnome could have told him that within fifteen seconds of meeting those two psychos. How is it that most of us are so spectacular at avoiding what is right in front of us? Is it stupidity or some sort of survival mechanism? I did vaguely realise when I moved to Sydney that I was drinking too much, but because I had absolutely no intention of stopping, I just couldn't let myself admit it. Along with working at night, it had also really screwed up my sleeping patterns, so I really couldn't get any shuteye without imbibing a lot; I couldn't risk the alternative. Who wants to be awake and sober in the middle of the night, with nothing to do but what I'd been avoiding – thinking?

Drinking pervaded every part of my life, pleasure and work. I don't know that I could've picked a career more conducive to being a lush. I really was able to convince myself that it was just all one wacky rollercoaster, and there's no doubting that I did enjoy myself. Slowly, though, it was becoming less about good times and more about something booze excels at – escape. It's the best way to forget about a show you may not have been happy with, a childhood you haven't really put to bed, or just something embarrassing you did because you were drunk. If you can just crawl to the part of the day when you can have that first drink, you'll be fine. And you'll be able to block out other people's judgments as well as your own. I didn't think about any of this, or the fact that maybe wanting to outrun parts of my life had always been in the background of even the headiest of days. Unfortunately, it also meant that I often forgot what other people told me. I once got drunk with a top chick that I worked with, only to have her say to me the following afternoon, 'Thank you so much, I've been needing to talk like that for a long time. I mean, I haven't told anyone about . . . well, you know, but that was just great advice.' Of course, I was standing there thinking, 'I haven't the slightest idea what you're talking about, but I guess if I suddenly see you at a lesbian gig or leaving an abortion clinic, I'll put it together.'

It's hard to see how I could increase my intake during my twenties, but I was heading for a pretty big revelation that would derail myself and my family for a long time.

Since moving to Melbourne, I hadn't had that much to do with my parents, but I did generally return to Perth for Christmas. At the end of my nerve-racking but successful year on *The Late Show*, I went back to WA foolishly hoping for a genuine summer holiday in the bosom of my family . . . and found out that I was adopted. My then sister-in-law decided to share the news with me after a particularly distressing family argument on Christmas Day. Season's greetings.

Many people seem to start 'searching' when life serves them up a shit sandwich. This didn't happen to me at the time, but I do wonder if it would have been different if I'd still believed in something when I found out that I wasn't biologically a

Lucy. And by something, I mean anything: crop circles, UFOs, Scientology, or whatever that thing is where people stick candles in their ears and burn them. I'd been dismissive of Mum's faith providing her any comfort when Dad had had his heart attack, but it was probably slightly more reassuring for her than my approach of 'life is meaningless, then we die – scull!'

Instead, I went on the overseas trip that I'd been planning for over a year, which was a huge mistake. The trip was always meant to be some kind of voyage of self-discovery, but now I was double as lost as I'd thought. Did I really think I was going to find myself in a holiday resort in Mexico? Surely, it would all fall into place for me in New York? London? Dublin?

Since I was re-evaluating everything, every time I watched a different television show my new choice of career would change. *LA Law*? Susan Dey looked hot as a lawyer. *St. Elsewhere*? Surely it wasn't too late to study medicine? Thank God, in London, I wasn't a fan of *Prisoner*. In the meantime, I pursued stand-up in England because I needed to make a living. I had to start from scratch, which meant returning to the types of gigs I'd been very happy to move on from back home. They were actually worse, because you often had to travel miles to get to them, with comics you didn't know, and when you arrived, you copped an extra layer of abuse from the audience for being Australian. This generally involved a reference to our propensity for sleeping with sheep. I mean we've all had our desperate moments, but as a woman I felt this would involve a level of commitment I lack. I mean, who hasn't fucked a chicken, but really, a sheep?

After a few months, I just thought, 'Forget it . . . I'm going home.' I probably don't need to add this, but on top of everything, I was drinking A LOT.

My self-esteem was pretty low. At one stage, I was living with a friend of a friend in Greenwich. Pip didn't have a television, so most nights we opted for another type of box to keep us entertained – cask wine! One night, my housemate answered the phone and gave out our address, looking a little like she'd just condemned her kidnapped child to being shot. When I asked her what the problem was she said that a minicab driver, whom she had no interest in, had asked for her number and he was now on his way over. This was bad enough, but Pip decided to go to bed TEN MINUTES after the cab driver arrived, leaving me to deal with the situation. There was no getting rid of him, so I had more to drink, and while we didn't have sex, we didn't exactly play canasta. The final humiliation came when he continued to ring for Pip, and when always told that she was out (often by Pip herself), he'd reply, 'Is the other one there?'

My trip lasted nine months. I was just glad to be home alive. Years later, my birth mother, Jan, would ask if anyone in my family had contacted me while I was overseas to see if I was okay. Until she asked the question, it had never occurred to me that they might have done (they hadn't), because we really weren't that kind of family and I wasn't even asking myself if

I was okay. I think I just thought that I should be getting on with it. I had some sense that I was depressed; I just had no idea what to do about it. By going overseas, I was hoping that something would happen to just snap me out of living how I was. In retrospect, it sounds fucking imbecilic, but I honestly thought that one day I would wake up and a job, or a partner, or SOMETHING would just make everything okay. And I had no idea what 'okay' was, either, I just knew this wasn't it. I really believed that adults – and I certainly didn't consider myself to be one at twenty-six – just had it figured out. They were responsible and had commitments and answers. They didn't go to parties and wind up throwing up on their own underpants (think it through, you'll work it out). On some level, I didn't believe that I had to do anything – it would just happen. I had no belief system, but I obviously had some sort of cuckoo idea that there was a key to life that got slipped under your door, maybe in your thirties. MY PARENTS WERE INSANE – WHAT WAS I BASING THIS ON?

I wasn't ready to stop my demented drinking but the later I got into my twenties, the more I was starting to have a sense that this was no way to live. I don't know that my friend Olivia felt the same way. There's no denying that my actions were self-destructive, but Liv took that phrase to a whole other level. At least I always had work to put some parameters on my boozing, but she didn't, and while having a child slowed her down a bit, it wasn't for long. I would always stop just before breaking anything from a limb to a tooth, but sadly my friend didn't. It was always a helluva ride with her, and generally a hilarious one, but what can appear 'wild and crazy' while you're young can start to look quite different as you get older, especially when your addictions go way beyond alcohol.

Obviously, Olivia wasn't only drinking because she was having a ball, either. She certainly had her own issues she was dealing with (like most of us, they involved her childhood), and her outward confidence and *joie de vivre* masked a hatred of herself that dwarfed everyone else's, including my own. It took me a long time to work this out.

Because I loved her so much, as well as idolising her, it was years before I saw that nothing was ever enough for my friend, with anything. She was never beautiful enough or thin enough, she could never drink enough and she could never ever get enough love. Whether you were a partner or a friend, she would push you and push you until often she got what she seemed to want: you walked away, confirming, as she had always believed, that she wasn't worth it.

I am honestly yet to meet an addict or ex-addict who isn't funny, smart and totally charming. Olivia had all these qualities in spades and when she shone her light on you, you lacked for nothing. I often wasn't really interested in men when she was around, or anything else, because I was having too good a time.

I still look back on those years as golden in terms of our friendship, even if I'm not altogether proud of some of my actions and decisions. I loved Liv as I've loved very few people, but I was about to hit a point that made me change course, while she wasn't.

Our friendship had also started to change slightly because, even though I was in an alcoholic haze, I was growing up and starting to see my pal's behaviour a little more clearly. But for many years, my idea of happiness was getting drunk with my best friend Olivia. I really felt that she was my soul mate and when I was drinking and laughing with her, I didn't have a care in the world.

And this was why I was able to slide all the bad stuff about booze under the carpet, because it was giving me two things I craved: getting outside my head and connecting with people. I mean, boy, had I found a way to RELAX. I wasn't watching myself when I was drunk, I was right there, not over-thinking anything, and, let's be honest, even two people who have absolutely nothing in common can bond by getting drunk together, so when you're with someone you actually do feel a connection with, it's bliss. You might not remember what you've talked about, but you know you've shared something, even if it's a hangover, and despite even a crippling one of those, you might judge yourself but you tend not to judge each other. (Well, unless, as was the case with an ex-boyfriend of mine, someone has dropped their pants and waved you goodbye with their penis.) And that's the thing with the people I know who are big drinkers. It's like a kind of club where the enormous glass house you're all in means that there's a level of acceptance. I trust the people I've been really drunk with more than the people I haven't, because in some ways they've seen me at my most vulnerable, not to mention my most incomprehensible, and they still like me.

4

BOYS

In my late teens, I may have been a devout Catholic but that still didn't stop me from checking out all the boys whenever our family went to mass. Because I went to an all-girl school and our family rarely left the house, this and the football field were my only opportunities to take a peek at the opposite sex. The pickin's were slim – unfortunately, the hottest guy in church was the semi-naked one up the front nailed to a cross. (I'm sure *that* image hasn't fucked with many peoples' heads.)

This was more than just hormones. Like most ladies I knew, I grew up believing that real and everlasting happiness obviously lay in meeting a cute guy. He may not have been hanging out at our local parish of Corpus Christi, but I never doubted that I would meet Mr Right and that he would simply solve all of my problems. He's turned out to be quite elusive.

Most of us became aware of the opposite sex at school (if you started dating at kinder, I don't want to know about it). They were either in your classroom or, if you went to a single-sex school like me, you encountered them at excruciating socials and blue-light discos. (My most vivid memory of one of these is of a boat cruise where almost every girl, aside from me, burst into tears when the Australian Crawl song 'Reckless' came on. At the time I put it down to the lyrics, but now I understand it was probably the realisation of just how limited the options were, in terms of suitors.) The one time an attractive boy tried to chat me up at some fancy-dress disco, I apologised to him for taking up his time and said that I would understand if he would rather be talking to his friends. I suspect that may have even put Gene Simmons off. It certainly sent this fifteen-year-old kid back to his mates. And so began my life as a femme fatale. My best friend in lower high school got all the guys – sure, she was a slut, but she seemed to know the secret language that males respond to. It may as well have been Esperanto, as far as I was concerned. It does also have to be said that while I would have loved a boy to ask me out, my main focus was still my marks. I figured there would be time for all this later, not knowing that, as was the case with alcohol, it's sometimes better to embarrass yourself at fourteen than for most of your twenties.

So I arrived at university a virgin. I desperately tried to hide the fact, although I suspect it would only have been more obvious if my vagina had placed a 'room to let' sign on the notice board: 'No previous tenants, owner slightly desperate, first-in, best dressed!'

Unfortunately, there really were only about three attractive

heterosexual men in the whole course. Looking back, I suspect that I may have had a couple of opportunities that I simply
missed through disbelief and inexperience. When I did finally
lose my virginity, at twenty-one, it was the result of the man
in question actually coming into my bedroom and starting to
take his clothes off. I remember thinking, 'Oh, I guess he's interested.' He'd spent the last hour putting his head in my lap – did
I think he was just TIRED?

I viewed men a little like salamanders: strange, scary and
something I wasn't entirely sure that I wanted to touch. The
truth was I just found the male species a bit terrifying because
I'd had so little to do with them. The two main men in my life
had been my big brother, who I'd worshipped, and my father,
who I'd tried to avoid, mainly because he wasn't around that
much, and while Dad could be fun, he was scary when he was
angry. So I had no clue how to relate to guys. Speaking to them
was an out-of-body experience – while my mouth engaged in
conversation, my mind was generally consumed by an inner
monologue that went: 'Did you really just say you've never
heard of Leonard Cohen?', 'Don't tell him that you don't know
what absinthe is!' and 'Why would you tell anyone that you like
zebras?'

So I truly marvel when I hear about people marrying in
their twenties, because for me, that decade's worth of romance
expressed itself as a combination of hopeless infatuations, a couple of short-lived ridiculous relationships and a dazzling array

of disastrous one-night stands, because I just didn't have a clue.

There were exceptions, thankfully. Such as the night I wound up sleeping with someone I liked very much, forcing me to concede that the feeling must have been, at least, a *little* mutual. I was so innocent it makes me cringe. He invited a bunch of us back to his place where many joints were smoked. I was the youngest there and I had probably had sex about twice and marijuana about three times. It didn't take long for me to be stoned out of my mind and mute with paranoia, although I do still remember laughing a lot, especially when our host re-entered the lounge room with lolly-filled show bags while wearing enormous tiger-foot slippers. The reason I stayed when everyone else left was not because I thought that I was in with a chance, but simply because I was incapable of moving. Finally, I said that I'd better call a cab, which is when the delightful gentleman in question said, 'Sure . . . Hey, look over there!' Of course, while I turned to look at nothing, he put his arm around me and that's when I finally realised I wasn't going anywhere.

I probably would've married this guy the next day but, regrettably, that was not on his agenda. He did, however, manage to make me feel quite wonderful the next time I saw him, simply by coming straight up and hugging me. As we all know, this is certainly not always how it plays out – I'm sure we've all encountered the person (I've probably been the person myself) who, despite the fact that the last time you saw them you were both nude, greets you a little like you're a stranger with a rare form of syphilis that can only be contracted by looking you in the eye and saying hello.

A slightly less fun one-nighter was the one where I wound up with such a spectacular case of stubble rash that I looked like a small lobster was sitting on my top lip. While *National Geographic* could have made a special on my mouth, there was no denying that it also looked like an outrageous case of herpes and it was difficult to explain to the women's collective with which I was meant to be devising a theatrical masterpiece. What was even more embarrassing was running into the perpetrator when my crayfish lip was at its height, to have him ask, 'Oh my God, did I do that?' just at the point when a mutual acquaintance came up and started chatting. Understandably, the newcomer's eyes were riveted to the bottom half of my face and finally he blurted, 'Jesus, what happened to your lip?' I found myself wondering, 'Mmm, what would Olivia Hepburn do?' Without saying a single word . . . I simply fled. I may have actually run, and no doubt it would have been straight into my next ludicrous encounter.

Many years ago, the quite excellent Kaz Cooke and I did a radio show called 'Foxy Ladies'. One week we decided to open the phone lines and dispense relationship advice. Our proudest moment was when a young girl rang us up wanting to know what she should do about a young man who was pursuing her, but whom she wasn't interested in. The problem was compounded by the fact that she was keen on someone else. We told her that she should just ask this other chap out and she reacted like we'd revealed that there was a way to turn a toilet paper roll into an iPhone. It had never occurred to her that she could choose. She rang back the following week to tell us that she was now dating the boy she really liked. Jesus, I wish someone had given me that advice, and I know I'm not the only one who fell into bed with a guy when they were younger simply because they'd had a go.

At least some of them were hot, such as the artist I met at my brother's wedding. He was extremely attractive and, disappointingly, also completely insane. At Niall's nuptials he came up to me and asked if he could put his hand up my skirt. I did my usual trick of playing hard to get and replied, 'Do you want to go outside?', whereupon we rolled around for a good hour. By the time I got up to make my best man's speech, I had lipstick smeared across my entire face and was completely covered in grass seeds. The 'speech' consisted of me slurring, 'Let's toast the spunky couple!' I guess I had other things on my mind – thank God I got another chance at Niall's second wedding.

The painter and I got a lift back to his place in the back of a ute, in which we continued to lovingly wrestle. I can't imagine what we both looked like by the time we arrived at his abode, but it certainly wouldn't have fazed his housemate, Pete the Greek. Pete was a Perth 'identity' who supposedly hadn't washed in twenty years. He was an extremely tall man who got around in platform shoes, flares and a witches hat (I swear that

I'm not making any of this up). From what I could gather, he watched television most hours of the day, while drinking many cans of beer, and, when the opportunity presented itself, would ask women to show him their breasts. I have seen some truly filthy houses in my time – the one I grew up in, for a start – but nothing will ever compare to the squalor these two lived in. Even now, the thought of that lavatory makes me nauseous. Somehow I managed to avoid it. I would happily have let my bladder burst before I went within two metres of that black hole. It was straight out of a ring of Hell in Dante's *Inferno*. Although I'm guessing even Satan occasionally pulls out the Toilet Duck.

Fortunately, my lover didn't live there for too much longer and we were able to conduct our affair within the harmonious and beautiful walls of a men's hostel. My gentleman would sit on the roof and stare at the sun, convinced that it was giving him special powers. I was so besotted that I remember trying it too, until I simply couldn't see.

I only ever saw this guy when I visited Perth and I don't know if he was unstable, 'artistic' or just one of those people who drank a lot and took copious amounts of drugs, but really, would have been off his rocker on half an egg sandwich. I finally had to admit to myself that it was probably not the 'relationship' I was after the night he told me how sorry he was about some awful news I'd recently received, and then tried to put his hand down my pants.

Not surprisingly many of these early encounters with men

involved a lot of booze, but that's what pretty much everyone I knew was doing. You'd go to a pub, meet a guy, get hopelessly drunk together and sleep with him. This would all then be discussed in excruciating detail with your girlfriends, which was often a lot more fun than the event, mainly because the sex was often just completely hopeless. Strangely, alcohol and lack of experience are not always the best combination when it comes to the art of lovemaking and, of course, we didn't grow up with readily available porn, so regrettably I still had pubic hair and no-one was giving me anal before coming in my face.

Finally, when I was twenty-nine, I dated an older man who actually knew what he was doing with his penis. That's right, I had my first vaginal orgasm and it was a little like the night I discovered a friend had some amyl nitrate in his freezer and I just couldn't leave it alone. (He told me that I'd wind up with a blinding headache and a lot less brain cells. 'Who cares?' I said. 'Who'd want to stop doing this?' How ridiculous! I never got a blondingg hodaike.) Unfortunately, the guy ended it after five months and stopped having sex with me after three. He was an ex speed addict with some issues, who told me that he broke up with every woman after three months and it was a testament to how much he liked me that he'd tried to stick at it for another two. I can't complain – he was a nice guy and he'd left me with some pretty nice memories.

This really was a turning point for me. I finally understood what all the fuss was about with the ol' horizontal folk dancing, and since then I've always found it pretty fascinating. Sex must be the one act humans perform that can be everything from a fantastic display of love and intimacy to something so horrible people can be imprisoned for it. When I was about thirty, I even paid for it. The experience wound up becoming one of my better-known routines. It was one of those things that came up in conversations with girl buddies frequently: 'Oh, if only we could all go to prostitutes like men . . . all I want is some decent sex.' So, one day I just did it. I think I wanted to see what it would be like to have sex purely for the sake of having sex and, admittedly, it is one of the few times in my life that I've deliberately done something thinking that I might get some material out of it.

Over the phone, the escort had told me that he looked a little bit like Russell Crowe, which is certainly not my type, but better that than Bud Tingwell (would have been just a little old for me). He came around to my place and he *did* look like Russell Crowe, as I liked to say in the routine, 'if the actor was shorter, older and had a pumpkin instead of a head'. I'm being unfair – he wasn't unattractive, but the sex was like a one-night stand that cost me six hundred and forty eight dollars. The only thing he did that was new for me was carry me to the bed, which made me feel like Deborah Kerr in the movie *An Affair to Remember* after she's been crippled.

One of the more enduring memories I have of the evening is of him opening his briefcase to reveal every sex toy imaginable and . . . a credit card swipe. I thought, 'Why is the swipe the only piece of equipment he's getting out for me?'

When I mentioned, extremely politely, that I was a little taken aback by how much it had wound up costing me, he seemed genuinely hurt, which was a little difficult to take seriously as he was, at that stage, wearing nothing but a skivvy. He looked like a fisherman who certainly had his tackle but not his trousers.

The most fascinating aspect of turning this into a routine was the number of men, strangers and friends alike, who wound up telling about me their experiences with sex workers and mostly, they admitted how depressing they'd found it. (There was also the Englishman who told me about a threesome he'd had in a spa. I've never met a guy whose face looked more like toxic raw mince and the thought of him having sex with just one woman – or even an inanimate object – was really a lot more than I could bear.)

I certainly wouldn't do it again. I have no doubt that there are many men who bang hookers regularly and have the time of their lives. I also did some talkback radio on the subject where I heard from a number of women who'd also not only heartily enjoyed themselves but, financially, had received much better deals. However – and the feminist in me hates to admit this – I seem to want something more than just an orgasm.

In my twenties, I think I believed that you just kept having sex with guys until eventually one of them would say, 'Oh, before you go and throw up again, I should probably mention that I'm "the one". That's right, I've arrived, and I'm going to complete you.' I genuinely spent a lot of those years checking in Linda Goodman's astrology guide to see whether the Libra who had just left was my soul mate.

But again, the reality was that you got the job of being my boyfriend if you had a crack. If you also happened to be a charming, funny alcoholic, well, I couldn't get enough of you. Strangely, this often didn't pan out well for me. In my late twenties I fell very, very hard for one of the above. I believe it was the first time I fell desperately in love and I hope that explains some of what's to follow.

The whole experience was a little like the scene from the Steve Martin film *The Man with Two Brains*: he knows that Kathleen Turner is all wrong for him, so he asks his dead wife for a sign if indeed he shouldn't go out with her. There's thunder and lightning and the whole room shakes as her portrait revolves and a voice repeatedly screams, 'NO!' Steve Martin then says, 'Just any kind of sign . . . I'll keep on the lookout.' It's amazing how we can kid ourselves when we're convinced a person is the missing piece of our puzzle. I mean how could I resist this guy, considering the first time I realised he was interested was when he said, 'If you see me out to my car, we can have a pash.' (You can see what a sucker I am for a sophisticated pick-up line.) I went weak at the knees, despite his pesky wife and child. We had an affair as his marriage broke up and the only thing I will say in his defence is that he was an absolute mess, who promised me nothing because that's all he had to offer.

It was a long time before we actually had sex, and no, it didn't occur to me to turn him down, because the fact that I'd been attracted to him for years managed to cloud any kind of good judgment that I should've displayed. And not for the last time, either. For all the married ladies reading this, rest assured you could not hate me for this more than I have hated myself.

After we consummated our mistake, he announced that he was too guilty to ever do it again, but almost equally guilty that sexually he wasn't going to be there for me, so he tried to find me a prostitute (this was before my own adventure in this area). Touching as this was, as the story unfolded it turned out his plan was that he'd also hire himself a sex worker, the idea being that we would watch each other having intercourse with our respective escorts. I have no idea why they didn't include a similar scene in *Bridget Jones's Diary* or *Love Actually*. Come on, Richard Curtis: what romcom's complete without the leads watching each other banging a couple of whores? Surprisingly, I passed on the offer. Also maybe not so surprisingly, I later discovered that his crippling guilt had not stopped him from sleeping with several other women during this period.

The only sensible decision I made during that time was to refuse when he asked me not to go to the Edinburgh Fringe Festival, where I was booked to perform a one-woman show. We talked every day and probably the most extraordinary conversation was when he rang to tell me that he felt that he'd just been badly ripped off by a lady of the night (are you sensing a theme here?). Don't worry: I comforted him. The only part of this story that stops me from wanting to blow my brains out is that he then insisted on phone sex (something I find a little difficult to take seriously), during which I came and he didn't.

The truth was that he was going through something pretty awful and I simply managed to convince myself that once he was out the other side of it, we would be fine. Sure, I was completely delusional, but I think a lot of us have put up with outrageous behaviour because we've believed that it was temporary. 'Oh, he's not going to be a serial killer *forever* . . .' When I returned from Edinburgh, he sat me down to tell me that he now had many women friends and that, as opposed to our previous arrangement of him virtually living with me, I would now have to make dates to see him. I should probably mention that one of his newfound friends had stayed in my flat with him in my absence. I don't need to add that there was only one bedroom do I? Presumably they were sleeping head to toe.

I accepted all of this. You're probably waiting for the part where I asked him to set fire to my hair or take a crap in my mouth.

We went on a date a couple of days after I got back, which went swimmingly until we got back to my place, where he took a phone call that lasted about an hour. When he finally got off the line, he announced that he was going to have to go and see one of his other 'friends'. I pointed out that this was my date, to which he replied: 'I have to go, because we've tried to have sex a couple of times and I haven't been able to maintain an erection, so I really have to go around and sort that out.'

I DROVE HIM.

The good news was that I didn't have a car, or a licence. The better news was that this was the end of it for me, although I did make a ridiculous effort to be his friend. I have nothing against him – he's a troubled man and I hope he's happier now than he was then. I know I am.

One of my problems was – and again, I don't think I'm the Lone Ranger here – that I spent a lot of time trying to be what I thought the boy I was with *wanted* me to be. Just before Mr Erection broke my heart, he and I went out to lunch with my best friend, Olivia. While he was in the toilet, I gripped her arm and said, 'Oh my God, I'm just not being entertaining enough, am I?' I think I often felt that I'd become his (or anyone's) girl-friend by somehow lying on my job application and that I then had to keep pretending that I was a whiz with Microsoft Excel when I couldn't even turn on a computer. Although, I should admit that occasionally I could let my guard down to quite a spectacular degree. I once met this guy's mother after the two of us had been drinking all day. I insisted on the meeting, say-ing, 'No, you don't get it. I'm great with parents.' I have no memory of my conversation with this poor woman, but appar-ently I used the word 'cunt' as often as I would normally use the word 'and'. I think my subconscious could have chosen a more polite way of letting me know that the relationship was a huge mistake.

I was uncomfortable with men because I was uncomfortable with me. I thought I didn't even know how to put my hand on someone's arm. I seriously remember thinking, 'What are you doing? You're moving your hand like a raw chop – that's not how you should touch someone.' These inner monologues weren't just taking place with boys, but with everyone. There was not a single conversation I would have, even with a close friend, that I wouldn't repeat to myself and critique like I was Simon Cowell. 'That wasn't funny . . . Jesus, that made you sound like a wanker. God, maybe I really am a wanker, and honestly, again with the zebras?' Somewhere in the back of my mind, I always I thought I was just on the verge of receiving a phone call from a loved one, who would say, 'Actually, now that I've had some time to think about it . . . I reckon you're off the team. You're just not cutting it.'

As you can imagine, under these circumstances it's hard to relax with someone, and that's what I craved to be able to do. I mean, I knew that I could achieve this with alcohol but I wanted to be able to do it sober. Obviously, I did have moments like that with some of the boys I wound up with, and that's what I loved, the intimacy. I loved lying around naked with someone you really liked, laughing, sharing a cigarette and a drink, and talking about anything. In those moments the monologue was not going on in my head. In fact, I wasn't in my head at all. Maybe you're kidding yourself, but it feels like at those times it's two people who have let their masks slip and are just really sharing something. Then you fall in love and one of you dies of cancer. Whatever, I couldn't wait to have that all the time. And I think I believed that if I could have that, the feeling of just being myself and not worrying about it, I would be happy.

5

DEATH

On the day of my thirtieth birthday, I remember waking up fully clothed on my couch, surrounded by empty wine bottles and overflowing ashtrays, and thinking, 'Yep, I guess entering my third decade isn't going to change anything about my life at all.'

While I didn't think that I was going to turn thirty and wake up a different person – have a sudden interest in morris dancing, for example – I'd had a growing sense of wanting to get it together for a while. It had been four years since I'd found out that I was adopted. I'd met my birth mother, which had been great, and while my family was still a mess, I felt that I was slightly less of one. I was living in a nice flat, touring a lot and doing well financially, but I also knew that I wanted to get healthier. I wanted to lose weight and not feel crap all the time. I ate takeaway a lot, I smoked, I still drank way too much, and I really, really, wanted a boyfriend. I certainly had quite a lot on my 'to do' list.

But only twelve months later it seemed like I was going to make Oprah look like an underachieving try-hard addicted to horse tranquillisers. Suddenly, I had it all! The opportunities that I'd been hoping would drop into my lap – both professional and personal – did! I was actualising all over the damn place, without lifting a finger. I hadn't even had to miss an episode of *Party of Five*. I was offered a regular television job on *The Mick Molloy Show*, which was with people I loved and was well paid, I was doing the Edinburgh Festival for the second time, with a show I was particularly proud of, so I was convinced it would go well, and I'd become one of the first Australians to be invited to the Montréal Comedy Festival. Everything was coming up Lucy!

And there was one other thing that happened at the start of that year . . . I fell in love. He pursued me like I've never been pursued before, or since. He was perfect. He was a musician, the sex was great and we could talk for hours – there was only one thing that bothered me. Damn, what was it? He didn't snore, he wasn't obsessed with sport . . . oh, that's right – he was married with two children. Here we go again.

Clearly, this is not something that I'm proud of. All I can say is that this time it felt different; it never felt like an affair. It felt like two people who had genuinely fallen in love. Naturally, I kept expecting the whole thing to go belly up any second. One friend said, 'Maybe it won't. Maybe this really is it, maybe you should really give this a try.' And when he left his wife – not because I'd asked him to – I did just that. I started to believe that this was one of those rare cases where two people really are meant to be together. What was also different was that this guy did promise me something: he told me and, whenever he could, my friends that he wanted to spend the rest of his life with me.

So at the start of 1999, I thought that I was embarking on one of the best stages of my life. One thing I might have asked myself was why, with all of this love and potential success, was I still drinking like a woman possessed? I obviously thought that it was just 'happy drinking'.

The night before I left for Montréal, the first episode of *The Mick Molloy Show* went to air. (I was able to leave because the idea was that I'd do live crosses from Canada and, later, Scotland.) Between packing and lovemaking (there's a fun visual for you), I had no time to consider how the television show had done – it would turn out, in the critics' eyes certainly, it hadn't done that well.

No matter. Very early the next morning, my manager, Kevin, and I boarded our flight to one of the world's most prestigious comedy festivals. We thought it would be a good idea to drink and take sleeping tablets while on the plane. At one point I was conscious of the fact that we were having a conversation while both wearing our headsets (i.e., we were screaming at each other). We also agreed to meet a total stranger at the Davis Cup, who was going to go to some trouble to organise tickets for us. You have no idea how much Kevin and I still hope that we live the rest of our lives without ever seeing this gentleman again. Without a doubt, though, the real triumph of the flight was somehow winding up in the cockpit. Kevin was in charge of a small camera that we were meant to use to film extra stories for Mick's show. I have no idea who was foolish enough to let us into the head of the plane – maybe nobody did, maybe we were simply trying to hijack it. All I recall is Kevin pointing the camera while I tried to get the pilots to say, 'You're watching *The Mick Molloy Show*.' What gripping viewing that would've made. I have no idea if someone finally asked us to leave but I'm hoping I didn't wind up sitting on the captain's lap and trying to fly the plane.

We finally landed at LA airport, still both pretty drunk. As we were going through customs there was an announcement instructing us to report to the nearest security guard. We had no idea why. I remember thinking that if one of the pilots wanted to ask me out, he should've just taken down my number. Before we knew it, we were surrounded by half a dozen very serious-looking men with guns, telling us that it was illegal to film in a cockpit. I'm sure a lot of espionage agents use the 'drunken Australian idiots working for a comedy show' cover. I remember a man yelling at me, 'Have you ever seen a movie where they show the cockpit?' I figured that this was not the time to mention *Flying High*, although the shit really did hit the fan. They confiscated our videotape, which probably only had footage of one of the pilot's elbows and maybe my ear. Thankfully, this was all before 9/11, so we didn't wind up in Guantanamo Bay or dead.

This incident pretty much set the tone of our Montréal trip, during which we were largely drunk, out of our depth and fairly useless. Kevin can now do this festival in his sleep, but back then neither of us had the slightest idea how to negotiate this microcosm of North American comedy. I certainly didn't leave with a sitcom deal under my arm. I think the experience was best summed up by the closing night dinner, attended by all the comedians. I was the only person not at a table of stand-ups; I was seated next to a duo of Chinese acrobats and a dwarf.

Although, I did meet Luke Perry (the 68-year-old who played a high-school student on the truly dreadful television show *Beverly Hills, 90210*). He came up to me after my spot on one of the comedy galas and told me I reminded him of his wife. She has curly brown hair and is English. I suspect that a lot of Americans think that if they can understand you and you're obviously not from their country, then you must be British. I'm constantly being mistaken for Helena Bonham-Carter or Rufus Sewell.

Edinburgh wasn't much different: I felt like I would've been better off spending three weeks learning how to make sushi. My show received good reviews, but there was no interest from English agents or producers, or even the pleasant discovery that people from the UK found me amusing, because, God bless them, the majority of my audience was Australian. I don't know why I wasted money on theatre hire when I could've just per-formed at the local backpackers' and led everyone in a medley of Cold Chisel songs.

But that wasn't all. Calls from home seemed to indicate that neither *The Mick Molloy Show*, which was rating poorly, nor my relationship were going well, and I wasn't in a position to do much about either. My man was on the phone daily telling me how devastated he was about leaving his wife and children. I understood this completely but didn't feel that it was the home-wrecker's job to say, 'You're right . . . I'm not worth it.' Even though, in truth, that's how I felt. Who wouldn't? A close friend, who'd been privy to my amour's protestations of life-long love, kept assuring me there was no way he was going back, but I had a sinking feeling they were wrong. Actually, I was starting to feel like a certain cruise ship that was responsible for the bulk of James Cameron's fortune.

The day I returned from Edinburgh, *The Mick Molloy Show* was axed, and a couple of months after this my relationship ended. Of course, Mick called to tell me – my guy just didn't contact me for three weeks and let me work it out for myself. When I eventually saw him I can honestly say that I would have gotten straighter answers out of a politician on wacky baccy. I knew that his children meant the world to him and I'd often said that I would completely understand if, for that reason alone, we couldn't be together. All I'd asked for was honesty, but (I now realise) how could I expect him to be honest with me when he clearly hadn't been honest with his wife? They're no longer together, but how had I wound up in that position again? Because I was in love. I had no idea what I was doing and I think

I was just in complete denial. I really had managed to block out the sound of warning bells because I just wanted it to work. I was heartbroken. For God's sake, I'd even let this guy feed me in a restaurant – it must have looked like I was recovering from a stroke.

Once I was newly unemployed and single, it just made sense to take my latest stand-up show to Perth and see my parents. I mean, whatever went wrong when I did that?

My family never really discussed the fallout from the adoption revelation, so we never really recovered from it. My mother's health went straight downhill after that Christmas and when I saw her again it was considerably worse. My father, whose own health was not great (despite a massive heart attack over a decade earlier, his love of drinking and smoking had remained largely unchecked), had become her constant carer. On one level, they seemed to have finally achieved some sort of peace in their relationship. They'd stopped screaming at each other. But it was also clear that Dad, robbed of all independence by my mother's reliance on him, was depressed and, I now think, a little out of his mind.

As a result, he and I had a falling out over something that barely makes sense: essentially, he was offended by a joke of mine about testicles. I explained that I had been referring to a friend's father's nuts but it made no difference. Something that, in the past, would have made this man with a great sense of humour laugh, resulted in him severing all contact with me and, subsequently, his son and grandson. I like to think that we would've worked it out, but I'll never know as six weeks later he died.

This meant my brother and I had little choice but to put our mother in a home, where she died ten months after our father.

So, in a little over a year, my entire life went to shit.

Most of us have lost jobs and endured breakups, and while they're no day at the beach, you can't put a profile on eHarmony and find yourself another set of parents. When they die, it's a life-changing experience and you just don't get it until it happens to you. When I saw my old best friend Michelle just before Dad's funeral, the first thing I did was apologise for my reaction at the death of her father when we were in our teens – I just hadn't understood. I'd given her a card with cartoon turkeys on it, for Christ's sake.

It doesn't matter whether you had a good or bad relationship with your parents: they're gone. If it was good, then you'll miss them like no-one else; and if it was bad, then you'll never be able to make it better. Unless we go first, it's one of the few certainties all of us will have to face – losing the people who brought us into the world and who probably had the single greatest effect on us. You don't just grieve for them, you grieve for yourself and your childhood. It brings home your own mortality, and makes you look at who you are now and what happened when you were growing up. Like nothing else, it makes you ask, 'Oh God, what went wrong?' It did for me, anyway.

Death had never really touched me until this point. Someone I'd been close to at university had died in a motorbike crash while I was overseas, but I hadn't seen him for a while so it took a long time for me to realise that he was really gone. But I do remember thinking, 'This is the beginning of losing people; this will be the first of many.'

When Mum and Dad died, I particularly remember thinking a couple of things: firstly, that I loathed the Catholic Church (I dealt with two priests during this period, and one was insufferable and the other a thief), and secondly, that my parents' lives had been a complete waste of time. My father had enjoyed some superficial pleasures, like smoking, drinking and extramarital pussy, but died estranged from both his children and clearly miserable. Mum had been deeply frustrated and unhappy for most of her life. In the later years, they had reached some sort of understanding, largely because my father seemed to view his new carer role as a kind of penance and finally gave my mother the attention she'd been craving from him for years. This would have made her happy but, as the song says, 'Is that all there is?' Then again, what the hell did I know? How well had I really known them, and how could I possibly judge their lives when I had no clue about my own?

More than anything when they shuffled off, I longed for some sort of feeling of intimacy. I remember, a few months after

Mum died, being at a wedding, desperate to sleep with some-one – and not in my usual happy-go-lucky way! Thankfully, the only possible contender was so self-involved that, despite the rumours of his enormous cock, I had just enough good sense to take myself home. I knew it wasn't sexual frustration that was motivating me – it was grief. As far as I can tell, this is a pretty common reaction – maybe because you've lost someone you love, you want to be convinced that love is still out there, that you can feel close to someone else, even if it's just physically. Or maybe you just want to be momentarily distracted. Fortunately, on this occasion, I realised that no matter how diverting this man's penis might have been, it would not have made me blind to the fact that he was just a bit of a tool.

I don't know how conscious I was of it at the time, but I think part of my distress came from not really understanding what had been lacking in my parents' lives. Of course they'd endured disappointments and ill health, but they had each married someone they loved, they'd had children who weren't serial killers, Dad had largely enjoyed his job and they both got some solace out of their religion in the end. They'd even seen Claremont win a grand final, but none of these things had been enough.

I wasn't there when either of them died but I actually 'talked' to them a lot after they departed. I still do that occasionally, even though I mostly believe I'd be better off talking to a couple of sock puppets. It sounds so bloody obvious, but when they go, the conversation really is over. There were so many things that I would never get to ask them. I was really just talking to myself and trying to make some sense of it all, I suppose.

Actually, considering how drunk I was, maybe I really was just talking to a sock. Their deaths didn't make me suddenly yearn for an afterlife – I wasn't aware of their absence making me yearn for anything. Although, I now know that it did.

My next involvement with death was very different. About five years later, my friend Lynda Gibson died. This will sound a little unhinged, but while her death at forty-seven was completely tragic, something about the whole experience wasn't.

Denise Scott, Lynda Gibson and I had written and performed a show called 'Comedy is Not Pretty' in Sydney, Adelaide and Melbourne, and I cannot say just how much I enjoyed working with those two hilarious, talented women. The show was a combination of stand-up, sketches and cabaret, with the overall theme being that life as a funny lady sucked. A highlight was a full-on physical fight that the three of us would have every night, complete with scathing insults. To give you an idea of the spirit in which the show was conceived, we wrote our own jibes for the others to throw at us. The lines were so personal that we always got gasps, as I don't think the audience realised the only person we were really being horrible to was ourselves. For example, one of the lines I wrote for Lynda to scream at me was something like 'Christ, Lucy, will you ever stop banging on about being adopted?' Ouch – if this book's anything to go by, I guess not!

We decided, a few years later, to write a sequel: 'Comedy is Still Not Pretty'. In the interim, our friend Lynda was diagnosed with ovarian cancer, so this show was a lot more confronting, for the people who paid to see it, but also for us. (Although one of the lighter reasons for this was the fact that we performed the whole show in nude suits. They were essentially flesh-coloured leotards where we had drawn on nipples, pubic hair and a bum crack with a black texta. Flattering is not the word I would use to describe them, so I don't know if this was more difficult for the audience to endure or for us. Actually, it was just difficult for Denise and me – somehow, Lynda managed to look hot in hers. Even the woman who had given birth to me said, 'You know, there's nothing wrong with your figure, but that outfit really isn't doing you any favours.')

One of the 'sketches' in the second show involved Denise and I arguing over who would give the eulogy at Lynda's funeral. The person who came up with that idea was Lynda. The day she came in with the script to share this with us, I don't think anyone, including our director, Col, could look her in the eye. She had been in remission but the cancer was back and I think we all knew that we might not have very much longer with our friend. Lynda would sometimes talk about touring the show, and again, Denise and I wouldn't know where to look.

I cannot tell you how proud I am of that piece. It was difficult, but wonderful. And it was an honour to share that last production with Lynda. I don't want to say that she was brave – only because she'd hate it – but sometimes we'd look at her during a rehearsal or on stage and just know she was in incredible pain. The audience wouldn't have had a clue. The show was in April and she was dead eight months later.

Lynda, her partner Al and their great friend Sal did something extraordinary in the last few months of her life: they threw their home open to all of their friends. Scottie described it as a house of love, and it was. There were always people around and my memory of that time is full of talking and laughing. We all knew what a privilege it was to be there, sharing those last weeks and days with Lynda.

Although both my parents (especially my mother) had been ill before they died, in a way they still went unexpectedly, so I'd never really experienced being there and sharing the inevitable with a group of friends. I had no idea it could be so positive. Ms Gibson knew so many people and a lot of us were finally able to put faces to the names we'd heard many times. She'd always talked to me of a friend called Madge, who's adopted, and said, 'You two have to meet and swap stories.' We finally did, sitting on a blanket on the lawn of the House of Love, only hours before Lynda died. Often when we speak now, we acknowledge how our great buddy was bringing people together until the very end of her life.

I don't know that any of us would have predicted this extra-ordinary time. I hope Lynda wouldn't mind me saying that she could be a little . . . shall we say, negative? There was an anger in her about the injustices of the world. I was terrified of Lynda when we first met, because I always felt that I might inadvertently say the wrong thing about a cause or issue. What was amazing was that if ever there was an injustice to be angry and negative about, it is surely when you know you're dying prematurely – but in the face of The End, all of that evaporated. Confronted by her own mor-tality, Lynda somehow became a beacon of light. The only thing I know for sure is that she wound up believing that God is love, and this seemed to help her arrive at a kind of peace in the face of death that I wouldn't have believed possible if I hadn't seen it. I don't think she meant God in a Christian sense, I think she meant that love is simply what it's all about. I can't tell you more about how she got there – I don't know that she said anything more concrete – but there was a light in her eyes that seemed to come straight from her heart. As with my parents' deaths, I didn't draw any firm conclusions from the experience about how to live your life, other than that it is possible to find grace in the most graceless of circumstances. Again, I have no idea how consciously this experience affected me, but at the very least it must have made me realise that death (and possibly life) did not have to be entirely about grief and regret.

Not surprisingly, it was a wonderful funeral and, in the end, Scottie and I gave one of the many speeches together.

Even though this time I was there to see it happen, I found it hard to believe that Lynda was gone. Then again, I never thought that I'd turn out to be adopted, or that *Hey Hey It's Saturday* would return to our screens. We actually know that the only certainty in life is death and yet not only are we shocked when people die, we're also surprised when the unexpected happens – yet it seems to me that life is a series of just those unexpected events. I only recently heard the line, 'People make plans and God laughs'. Are we just a pack of idiots?

Olivia wasn't really around when my parents died, and was completely absent during Lynda's death. A couple of months before my father had his fatal heart attack, my friend Sue and I had dropped her off at a rapid detox clinic. We picked her up afterwards and took her straight to Sue's place in the country. It was really only then that I understood what a massive problem she now had with heroin. A few years earlier, I'd been in Perth when she'd rung to tell me that she'd tried it for the first time. She sounded almost triumphant. I reminded her that she'd once said to me, 'You know, I should never try that drug because I think that I would just love it.' I'd hung up on her.

She was introduced to it by an addict that she'd fallen madly in love with, although I suspect that she was always going to find it in the end. Liv had clearly been very good at being secretive about it since, but I'd obviously been just as good at looking the other way when it came to her growing dependence. Back at Sue's, as my best friend fell in and out of consciousness (the treatment involves being heavily sedated), she told me things about the previous two years that made me realise she'd been virtually living a double life. Even in this state, she reared up at one point and said, referring to my recent dumping, 'Yes, Jude, but did he ever make you laugh?' And you know what? He hadn't. Liv and I used to tell each other everything and I believed that we would get back to that. I naively thought that this treatment would be the end of it all and that she'd be okay. It certainly didn't occur to me that things could get much worse.

Some time later, I realised the main problem was that Liv didn't really want to stop. She didn't even seem to think she really had an issue. This might all sound ridiculous coming from someone who was also pretty spectacular at burying their head in the sand, but, in my experience, few drugs are as insidious as heroin. I don't doubt that there are people who just dabble with it and are perfectly happy, and I also don't doubt that there are some perfectly functional addicts who have never told a lie in their lives, but for my friend, at any rate, it certainly brought out a side I hadn't really seen before. It's another cliché, but I think the fact that Liv came from a privileged background meant that the seamier side of this scene was also appealing. It was as if, when my buddy started taking this drug, she made a secret pact with herself, where she said, 'I am going to fuck up my life as comprehensively as I possibly can.'

I should possibly mention that I tried heroin a number of years before Liv did and, thank God, I hated it. But isn't that just the luck of the draw? It made me feel like I was about to be operated on. I remember lying on the ground unable to speak, feeling like I was at the bottom of a swimming pool, with the added joy of needing to vomit at regular intervals. I've always enjoyed social drugs that make you believe you're having incredibly in-depth conversations. I'm sure this is largely bullshit and that you're just chewing the inside of your mouth off, but it at least feels like you're experiencing something with others, even if it's just how foolish you feel because a moment ago you said, 'I don't think these drugs are working at all.' Heroin always seemed lonely to me. Although far from making Olivia nod off, it seemed to energise her – you might have thought she had taken speed, not smack. But she clearly still loved its anaesthetising effects – she said it was the best ever way to deal with a hangover. Beroccas might have been less damaging. Heroin must have given her the kind of relief that made booze seem like cordial. From what I can gather, it's a great time killer – not only do you have to set up the deal, but as Lou Reed says, 'you always gotta wait'. So I would imagine that even when you're not on the drug, it's still pretty much your main focus. My pal had found a pretty stupendous way to not think about any aspect of her life that bothered her.

The problem continued to escalate over the next five years, with regular trips to various rehab clinics, but the results were always short-lived. Neither Sue nor I were 'tough love' types, but we had both reached a point where we had to sit Olivia down and tell her she couldn't go on as she was, especially as she had a young son. Her behaviour had become increasingly erratic and the constant lies were frustrating and depressing. In the same week, Sue and I wrote Olivia letters telling her that we loved her, but also making it clear that she had to stop trying to deceive us and herself. We didn't care about the heroin, we said – what we cared about was that our friend was in such denial about her state that it was impossible to have any kind of real conversation with her. She had shut just about everyone else out of her life and it looked like we were about to join that list.

Really, I should have understood. I'd never wanted to admit that I was drinking too much because that would have meant that maybe I should do something about it, and you don't want to stop doing the thing that is so neatly blocking out all your other problems.

Olivia certainly had problems, although I honestly believe she could have done anything she turned her hand to. Her letters could have been published and her art was wonderful. She would print images and text onto huge canvases; the work was often self-referential and sometimes very funny. She could turn a can of three-bean mix, some rice and a tomato into a gourmet meal, and if she'd tried my profession, I think she would have cleaned up. But I don't know that any amount of praise or affirmation from strangers and friends alike could shut up the relentless cruel critic in her head – only smack could do that.

While my friend had many things going for her, she was also dealt some difficult cards. One of the more distressing problems Liv had had to endure, several years into her addiction, was a bout of a very rare kind of cancer. She was lucky enough to be completely cured, but it was an awful time for her. Many of her friends hoped that this reprieve might have been a wake-up call, but she wound up getting a number of those and heeded none. Instead, they generally became another reason to get off her head. Olivia never responded to my letter.

Someone who was there for her during this time of ill health was Lynda Gibson, who regrettably by that stage knew something about cancer. Olivia made no attempt to see Lynda before she died, which was so unlike the friend I used to know, although I refused to believe that she was completely gone. The day after Lynda's funeral, I moved to Sydney to begin the least spiritual part of my life – I started a job on commercial breakfast radio. I was upset I hadn't heard from Olivia and, at my then partner Collin's suggestion, I rang her. Her little boy picked up the phone, so there was no dodging the call. I listened to her heartbreakingly familiar litany of excuses and apologies, along with her protestation that we 'were sisters' and that she was going to sort this out by coming up to Sydney to visit for a couple of weeks. I knew that most of what I was being told was a lie, but still felt that there was some hope for my friend and me. It was the last time we ever spoke. Over a year ago, when post-production had finally finished on the TV show *Judith Lucy's Spiritual Journey*, my friend Olivia died.

In the seven years since we spoke on the phone, I had heard snippets from different sources about her life. While it was unlikely someone would have told me about the great times she was having, the reports I heard were never good. On a couple of occasions, we even passed each other in the street and neither of us uttered a word. What would we have said? Let's catch up sometime? There was nothing to say. We'd loved each other and known each other so well, yet ultimately our lives had taken very different turns. Our positions could so easily have been reversed. Maybe in a parallel universe, she's the comedian and I'm the one whose heart failed at forty-seven after so many years of abuse.

And when we were friends, she was the one who was interested in spirituality. When we were at the height of our drinking, she told me that one evening she had seen an incredible white light at the end of her bed that filled her with love and wellbeing. I thought she was pissed. Olivia was reading texts in her twenties that I wouldn't discover for another couple of decades, yet somehow I began to pull myself together and she died. I have no idea why I was the lucky one, but maybe I'm not – maybe she's somewhere having a ball. I hope so, because I don't know that she had one when she was alive.

For days after I heard the news of her death, I was just furious. I was so angry at this incredibly talented woman for having pissed everything away. Then I was just unspeakably sad. I think of her often.

It seems to me that most of us only ever question our lives when they slam us against a wall and fist-fuck us. (I'm old-fashioned: I think fists should be used for making war, not love.) Most of us only ever examine our behaviour when we're confronted by sickness, heartache, disaster or death. Birth is probably our only experience that is both good and life-changing. Generally though, only truly gut-wrenching moments seem to alert us to the fact that we might die too and that maybe we'd better try and work out what on earth the point of it all is.

My first encounter with this life-changing business was when I found out that I was adopted. This should have taught me two lessons: alcohol is not a healthy or wise coping mechanism, and straight denial is the same but less fun. I didn't want to face feeling angry, or sad, or uncomfortable in any way about what had happened to me, so I drank and locked it all in a cupboard. Who would ever have guessed that that approach wouldn't work? I should have written a book about healing and coping with grief simply called *Just Repress and Drink!* And when I had the horrible twelve months or so that culminated with my parents dying, I should have written the sequel, *Just Repress and Drink . . . Again!*

The day my father disowned me, by fax, I was due to perform that night and experienced the first of many panic attacks on stage. Logically, I knew the fears I was going to faint or wet myself in front of an audience made no sense. I hadn't had to wear a nappy in years, but logic plays no part in severe anxiety. The fears always seem completely real and, much worse, totally beyond your control.

Considering this, it really was a stroke of genius that only months after Dad died, therefore preventing any reconciliation, I toured a one-woman show about my *annus horribilis*. It was called 'Colour Me Judith' and actually involved an entrance with me GETTING OUT OF A COFFIN, which I was sealed in for some time before the show started. I could really only have made the whole experience more relaxing by being buried alive. And, to finish it off, Mum fell off her perch before I'd made my way around the nation – so the later performances had a bonus ending!

Not surprisingly, I spent the year in an alcoholic daze. I have absolutely no idea how I got out of bed every morning. At least before the adoption news, I'd mainly had a good time when I was three sheets to the wind, but there was none of that now. I can't tell you how many nights after the deaths of my parents I spent getting stoned as well as drunk and watching hour after hour of crap television (another lifelong addiction). So often, I remember thinking, 'Thank God, only three more hours and I can go to bed.' I just didn't want to be awake.

I could also no longer deny that my lifestyle had been

affecting my health for some time. God knows how many natur-
opaths, acupuncturists and Chinese herbalists I've seen over
the years, with complaints about everything from never-ending
thrush to chronic digestion problems. I would tell them about
what was by then my reasonably healthy diet, but neglect to
mention that I really needed a chain gang of livers to cope with
the toxins I was also putting into my body. I would skip off with
a new batch of herbs after my cupping or massage, when I may
as well have just cut straight to the six pack for all the good they
did me.

An indication of my state of mind is that I often fantasised
about my own funeral. It would actually cheer me up. I would
enjoy thinking about the eulogies as I pictured a room packed
to the rafters, and I would fantasise about the many, many men
wandering around weeping and thinking, 'Oh my God, I was
just so in love with her and she was so very beautiful, and now
I'll never be able to tell her . . . I'll never be able to make love to
that incredible woman.' (My coffin would be wheeled out while
Lionel Richie sang 'Three Times a Lady'.)

Before writing this book, I was aware that for many years
I'd been stuck in a particular pattern. I was a heavy drinker and
dope smoker who could manage reasonably well until tragedy
struck, and then I would go completely off the rails. But only
writing it down has made me realise how grimly predictable my
behaviour was and how miraculous it is that I still have teeth.

I used to do a regular weekly spot on a popular radio program where I would talk about my life and drunken escapades. I now understand why one of the presenters told me that whenever they got letters about me, they all said the same thing: 'Is she all right?' How on earth did I keep convincing myself that I was? It's like I was wandering around in a cloud of smoke with a ringing alarm on my head, denying that my legs were on fire.

Here's yet another story that maybe should have indicated that I hadn't been on top of things for some time. Along with death, moving house is in the top five most stressful events we go through, so when Liv and I had to move out of the share house we had lived in with Michelle (she had already returned to Perth), we arranged NOTHING, except more to drink. What did we think was going to happen? A fairy was just going to sort it all out for us? All I remember about the days leading up to the move was drinking a lot of beer from about midday and taking valium like Tic Tacs. The night before the removalists were due, we went to a dinner party where I got so drunk I had to spend the night. Liv went home, then tried to return to the dinner party, without success, as we'd all crashed by that point, and she got back to our place the second time around dawn. She'd now locked herself out of the house and had to climb the fence. She fell into our back garden, got completely covered with dirt and then had to go straight to art school for her final-year assessment. In the meantime, I'd come home and started vomiting. The movers arrived around lunchtime and my friend instructed them to take her bed last, because that's what I was lying on in between lurching to the bathroom. My idea of packing was to put everything in garbage bags and, of course, we had put garbage in some of the garbage bags too. And so, inevitably, I took a bag of rubbish with me and lost virtually my entire wardrobe. And this is a story from what I consider to be the good times.

Nearly ten years after that incident I was finally starting to realise that alcohol was only compounding my problems, but what was the alternative? Work was driving me crazy, Mr Right had broken my heart and I had lost my best friend. I was adrift. I had nothing to fall back on, and I was completely miserable.

6

MAGIC HAPPENS

And then I realised what was missing – Jesus. So, I opened my heart and 'very truly, I tell you no-one can see the kingdom of God without being born again'.

Nobody panic – that's not what happened to me. But it did happen to my friend Lily when she reached rock bottom thanks to a raging heroin addiction. When I say 'rock bottom', I mean she'd stolen from people, lost her home and her child, and tried to commit suicide. I'm extremely grateful that Christ became her pal, or I might have lost another friend to that drug. Thankfully she's a Catholic now, so she's stopped waving her arms in the air like she's in an old Bay City Rollers' clip and looking like a halfwit.

I was certainly at my lowest point (to date) when my parents died, but I was still bathing regularly and I still got back to work. I certainly wasn't interested in killing myself. In fact, the only time I ever seriously entertained that thought was when I was travelling abroad just after I found out I was adopted.

That was probably because my beer gut made me look like a python who'd swallowed a small pig, and I also had shocking dermatitis, which made everything I wore look like the inside of a snow dome. Or it could've been because nothing, not even New York, the most exciting city in the world, could distract me from the fact that I felt my family was no longer my family and I'd been stupid enough to run away from my friends.

Even though touring was a struggle after my parents died, it did stop me from being permanently drunk, and at least my buddies were around. And looked out for me. I'd been having trouble sleeping and one night while working in Sydney I got a couple of sleeping pills from a Melbourne friend, Colin, who was also visiting the Emerald City. Regrettably, I decided to take them while we were still at his hotel, so by the time my other friend, Andrew, saw me back to where I was staying, I was virtually comatose. He left me in the corridor while he went down to reception to replace my key card, which no longer worked. By the time he returned, I was completely unconscious, so my poor friend had to hold the door open with one leg while grabbing one of mine and then pull me into the room. Another time, thanks to just liquor, my friend Warwick had to climb into a toilet cubicle to try and rouse me (we've never discussed how much of me he saw from the waist down and I believe that's how the relationship has survived), and apparently I was often dropped on the floor as friends would try to carry me to bed. My friend Jayne's favourite story is about when she decided to leave me passed out on a couch, even though my legs were at a ninety-degree angle, pointing straight up to the ceiling. This was my period of thinking I was a bracket.

My pick of the bunch is when I had a couple of buddies over one night and, after the requisite amount of alcohol, two of us decided to perform some interpretive dance. Unfortunately, this involved Colin, who was wheeling me around on an office chair, swinging me into a wall, and I cut my head open. I think the part of the tale that alerts you to what a tremendously dedicated performer I am is the bit where I kept dancing with blood gushing out of my skull. Happily, this was also when one of my neighbours decided (probably quite reasonably) to turn my power off, so Colin and his partner Dave wound up pouring half a bottle of vodka over my head while holding a lighter up to the damaged area. When I saw my birth mum and retired nurse, Jan, the next day, she was not impressed with my friend's handiwork and oddly thought that I should have gone to hospital. So as you can see, no rock bottom for me. I WAS FINE.

When I was sober, I was grief-stricken because my parents were gone, and I'd never be able to achieve the relationship I'd wanted with either of them. At the time, though, I don't remember thinking much about the meaning of life or even about changing my own. Sadness really simplifies things in a way; you just concentrate on getting through the day and, in my case, the location of the nearest bottle shop.

At one stage, the 'Colour Me Judith' tour (or, as I like to

call it, the 'I'm Completely Losing My Mind' tour) took me to Adelaide, and I'll always be indebted to a friend, Amanda, who took me out for lunch and made the very sensible suggestion that I do something about my health. She had been doing yoga for a while and thought that maybe I should try it.

I can't really explain why I agreed, and why it was at this point that I began to change path, or at least notice that there was another path a little further away from the gutter. Some tiny part of me wanted to pull myself out of the hole I was nose-diving into. Only a couple of years earlier, I'd been seeing a full-blown alcoholic and I knew that I didn't want to wind up like that. Maybe it's as simple as the fact that, even during the last year or so, I'd still laughed, I'd still had people show me that they cared about me and I still really cared about them. That's right, I needed people, I was one of the luckiest people in the world, and Barbra Streisand was right all along.

Believe me, this was not the point where I started living in an ashram, or even stopped using deodorant and took to wearing cheesecloth and open-toed shoes. This was just a little step forward; there were MANY steps backward to come.

I'd done yoga a handful of times before, but my irregular hours had been a great excuse not to commit to a regular class. My buddy simply pointed out the amount of money I was spending on things that weren't so beneficial for me (reading between the lines: booze and drugs) and suggested that I take a fraction of that and hire a yoga teacher to give me private lessons once a week. I'll always remember saying that I thought that seemed so self-indulgent. But even as I said it, some part of me knew that almost EVERY SINGLE ASPECT OF MY LIFE was pure self-indulgence. So when I got home to Melbourne, I looked up the Yellow Pages. I wasn't really aware of the spiritual side of yoga that day when I let my fingers do the walking – I was just thinking about getting a bit of exercise, maybe not hyperventilating when I walked up a small incline – but it's interesting I wasn't attracted to squash. It would turn out to be the best fifty bucks a week I ever spent.

Timing really is everything. For example, when I first saw *The Tree of Life* I thought it was a piece of shit, but the second time I saw it, I also thought it was a piece of shit. However, there are films, books, places, even people, that you can encounter at the wrong time and just hate or not get at all. But sometimes, if you get another chance, it can be a completely different experience and you can see them in a different and even positive light. And so it was with yoga. While I'd enjoyed the two or three classes I'd attended in the past, I'm sure another reason I'd never committed to it was that I associated it with the whole New Age movement and, for years, I'd been scathing of that whole bunch of Angel card, crystal-carrying nonsense, both privately and on stage. This was because the New Age world was not entirely foreign to me.

While Catholicism had been my only real experience of anything 'other-worldly', weirdly it was the biggest Catholic in the

Lucy family, Mum, who'd experimented with other forms of hocus-pocus. My mother was very smart but also very bored being a housewife, and that might have led her into experimentation. Or maybe she too felt that her religion was not quite the whole answer. I was dragged off to a transcendental meditation class with her at the age of eight and, over the years, she also had dealings with the Charismatic Movement, along with re-birthing and even yoga. As a small child, I found the meditation completely mystifying and thought her other explorations were as significant as her short-lived obsession with macramé, and at least we'd wound up with some pretty natty pot holders from that.

So for me, all this was tied up in one big garbage bag, and when I walked away from the Church, I walked away from the lot of it. The New Age lunatics I seemed to continue walking into only confirmed my intolerance.

The very first house I shared in Melbourne was owned by the mother of the brother and sister who lived there (boy, did they hold all the cards). At one point their mum came to stay with us and, while I have no doubt that she is a nice person, all her talk of visualising everyone in pink bubbles and sending them good wishes made me want to slap her repeatedly across the face. One afternoon, she asked me and her son, Robert, who was as big a sceptic as I was (he created paintings that simply consisted of words like 'hate' and 'poison'), if we could see her aura. Stupidly, we both said that we couldn't. So she nailed a blanket to the kitchen doorway, stood in front of it and insisted that we stare at her until we could see it. I realised, after about four minutes, that there was every chance that Robert and I could be sitting there for the rest of our lives, so I said, 'You know, I think I can see something,' secretly thinking that it was the steam coming off this enormous pile of shit.

In my late twenties, I had a very unpleasant experience with reiki. I still don't truly know what reiki is – I thought the word should only be uttered in a racist sketch about leaves. I'd just come out of a particularly stressful work experience, where I'd been grinding my teeth so much that I was starting to resemble a bulldog. A friend suggested that I should try some reiki with an acquaintance of hers. When I asked what it involved, she replied that it was a lot like massage, 'really relaxing'.

This reiki master knew a little about me and after only a couple of minutes asked if she could tell me a little bit about my past lives. She may as well have said that she wanted to chat about the Loch Ness monster, but let's not forget that I'm a comedian and I'm not one to say no to potential material. This woman knew that I was adopted and, apparently, 'saw' me and my birth mother as Jews during Nazi Germany, although Jan was cast as my father during this happy interlude, for some reason. Of course, we were being herded off to be gassed. The good news was that somehow Jan saved me, but the bad news was that I saw her being clubbed to death by Nazi soldiers. I remember lying there, thinking 'Who needs the Bahamas? This is like a holiday!'

I wound up telling this story on the radio and I often did material about the New Age. Let's face it, it's easy pickings, and I sought it out. I often had readings done or attended spiritual expos with the express purpose of taking the piss. I once had a 'sand reading' done that involved me plunging my hands into a bucket of dirt so that a woman could tell me this: 'I'm getting your guardian, her name's Marion, she's very keen on pot plants – are you keen on pot plants?'

'No,' I replied.

'She's telling me that you're about to start studying . . . ?'

'No.'

'Oh dear, she says that you're very worried about a medical condition . . . ?'

Three strikes you're out. I wanted to tell her that Marion was more likely saying that the next time I had twenty bucks to spare I should just jam it up my clacker.

I had my aura photographed. It was very yellow and made me look half lady, half pineapple. I read magazines like *Conscious Living*, which had an article that actually suggested that instead of the word 'vagina' we should use the phrase 'sacred space', and, my favourite, instead of 'penis', we should use the phrase 'wand of light'. Not surprisingly, Darth Vader was lurking in that punchline somewhere. I read books like *The Goddess in the Bedroom*, which advised women to use a cucumber instead of a vibrator, but added that they should also use a condom 'even though there's no sperm involved', because of pesticides. The jokes wrote themselves.

I also did a routine about an article that I'd read, entitled 'Manifesting Abundance'. It was comprised of financial tips from a group of spirits who'd been channelled by the authors and who were collectively known as 'Abraham', which, if nothing else, strikes me as downright slack – they couldn't be bothered coming up with another couple of Christian names? But this side of the New Age in particular has always made me angry. If you're so in touch with the universe, shouldn't you be concerned with helping others, as opposed to your bank balance?

And it's hard not to be cynical when a chain of stores that specialises in selling yoga clothing covers its bags with slogans like 'Friends are more important than money'. Then why are your outfits so expensive? Or, 'Do one thing a day that scares you'. How about robbing one of your stores? 'Children are like life's orgasms . . .' No. They're not. You can't fake one and if you put one in a pornographic movie, you'll be arrested. And finally, 'Dance, sing, floss, travel'. Fuck off.

What makes me even angrier are the corporations who have adopted New Age jargon ('love', 'essence', 'be here, now') to sell everything from cars to tampons. I hate to break it to you, but I don't think a shampoo is really the way to Nirvana. But maybe advertising companies feel this is justified because the dark side of all this searching can be a kind of selfishness. I read a great quote somewhere that said nobody goes to see a psychic to learn how to be more generous with other people.

I guess you can use anything to justify your behaviour. I once had a one-on-one class with a woman in Byron Bay who taught meditation. I knew virtually nothing about it and thought some guidance would be useful. The 'teacher' told me that it was all about letting go and this was something that she was applying to every aspect of her life, which was why she hadn't insured the brand-new car she'd recently bought. Unfortunately, she'd written it off almost immediately, but this was okay because now she just relied on the universe to get her to work. Sometimes she would be able to get a lift from her out-of-the-way house and sometimes she wouldn't, and on those days, she simply didn't turn up to her job.

'You're a lazy idiot,' I remember thinking. 'And I wish that I'd hired a coconut to teach me about meditation.'

Not that I hadn't enjoyed going down the self-absorbed path myself with the one friend I had who was into this stuff, the wonderful Sue, who never used her interest to try and make money but only to make those around her feel good. A boyfriend of mine laughed when Sue offered to do his astrological birth chart, but when she started telling him how creative and talented he was, he said, 'You know, this stuff is a lot more accurate than I thought.' My attitude was similar. I didn't really believe most of what she said, but it was great to have someone who wasn't a therapist talk about you for an hour.

So this was where I was coming from before my Adelaide friend told me that I should try yoga. The first class I'd been to had been with my drinking partner, Olivia, and my memory is that someone farted, we giggled like schoolgirls and never went again. The other couple of classes had left me feeling great but just weren't compatible with my drinking schedule. The yoga gods were certainly smiling on me when, after my buddy's suggestion, my search through the Yellow Pages led me to my first teacher, Melanie. Not only is she very good, but she's younger than me and, to be perfectly honest, the best thing was that she didn't mind a wine and would even have the odd cigarette. This probably isn't true of her now, but if I'd encountered a judgmental puritan at that point, I have no doubt I wouldn't have lasted more than a week.

Melanie would come around to my little flat, and from day one I loved the physical side of yoga. I'm sure that everyone has an activity that makes their body go, 'Oh my God, where have you been all my life?' I remember feeling like that. Seeing Melanie would always leave me in a good mood. My body would feel great because it was being used for something other than a toxins catchment area. Discovering new muscles might have not felt so wonderful the following day, but at the time all that stretching felt good. It was wonderful to be moving in a different way, or, let's be honest, at all. I had always felt completely physically incompetent. Mum had never really let me do sport at school, so I found anything other than walking a little confronting. Because I wasn't in a yoga class, I didn't have to worry about looking stupid and, unless my teacher was an extraordinary liar, I seemed to be better at it than just 'not terrible'. The classes always ended with some relaxation – or as I liked to think of it, lying on the floor without being drunk or watching television – and this all left me feeling full of energy and like I'd accomplished something.

I'm sure any kind of exercise is going to make you feel better if you commit to it. Yoga also made me feel happy because I was trying something different that was actually good for me. Whether I'd been happy or sad, for years my life had been a variation on the same routine – I couldn't think of the last time that I'd genuinely tried something new. And yet there I was. I'd actually been able to make a tiny, tiny change in my life, and that in itself had put a little spring in my step.

7

MORE COMEDY

So, very slowly, yoga became a part of my life. And I really do mean slowly, and a small part at that. Sometimes I'd go for weeks or months without doing it, because of work or benders. If time was ever a constraint, it was the first thing to go. If I was stressed or tired or not feeling very good about myself, why on earth would I do the one thing that actually made me feel better? That makes no sense! Far better to stick with the old habits that got me nowhere, if for no other reason than that they were familiar. I mean, thrush was familiar to me, and why would I want to shake that old friend?

But, very slowly, I was starting to realise what yoga practitioners meant when they talked about the body and mind being connected. I always came back to yoga and, more than that, it never occurred to me that I wouldn't. I never thought, 'Well, I've had more than enough of that bendy, breathing shit, maybe I'll try kickboxing.'

Three years after the death of my parents, as much by

accident but, I like to think, a little by design, I was certainly in better shape than I had been. That wouldn't have been hard – it was either that or start looking like Nick Nolte's mug shot. So when I was offered an obscenely well-paid job getting up at 4 a.m. to do breakfast radio in Sydney, it seemed like a great idea! I was still drinking and smoking dope every night, but moderately. (It's interesting how that term varies for everyone, isn't it? I thought a bottle of wine and four joints daily was virtually a health kick.) I was in a relationship with a lovely man, Collin. And I thought the discipline of early nights and five days a week working was just what I needed to really clean up my act. I would do yoga daily, I would be forced to be healthy and I loved the idea of getting away from stand-up, for which I was still struggling with panic attacks and anxiety. All up, it seemed a very sensible plan. I knew working for commercial radio might be a bit like sucking the Devil's cock, but I knew a lot of comics who had still managed to do really great work with Satan's schlong in their traps, so why not me? I'd also never really given mainstream a try and maybe I needed to do that too. I was in a good relationship, I hadn't thrown up in my underpants in a while and here was a job that could offer me success and financial security. Maybe those magical keys to life were about to be left in my letterbox? At thirty-six, I was finally going to have it all!

And I would get to work with one of my oldest and dearest friends, Kaz Cooke, as well as the thoroughly delightful Peter

Helliar and our hand-picked brilliant producer, Emma Moss. Really, WHAT COULD GO WRONG? It turned out, just about everything.

Possibly that should have occurred to me during one of the preliminary meetings, when management asked what we would do about audience response to the changing of the guard. We were taking over from a very popular team and, inevitably, the listeners would hate us for a while – people seem to struggle with change, no matter where they come across it. I said that I thought we should read out any hate mail we received and talk about it. 'Let's not try and pretend it's not happening,' I said, 'let's tell the truth.' That's when one of my bosses said, 'Honesty? I like it, what a great angle . . .'

The nature of commercial radio is that nothing – not the listeners, not the announcers, nobody working at the station – is as important as the sponsors. In other words, nothing is more important than making money. In my opinion, this doesn't bring out the best in people. Everyone seemed to walk around with an axe dangling above their heads, and maybe this is why some extraordinary behaviour occurred and was tolerated. I heard one story where, as a punishment for being late for work (the result of just sleeping in), a gentleman was not only demoted, but made to stand on the median strip outside the station holding up a sign declaring what an idiot he was. I have no idea if this is true, but if it is, why wouldn't he have just told them to fuck off?

It's an organisation that thrives on making people believe that their job is everything and that, no matter how miserable they are, no matter how underpaid or badly treated they are, it's somehow worth it. Many people start working in radio when they're in their teens and often their lives revolve entirely around the station, including being moved from city to city for work. They sometimes live with each other and often socialise together.

Maybe it's this bubble-like existence that explains how one day, desperate for ratings, management suggested that our team run a competition called 'Celebrity Sperm'. The idea was that the woman who won would get to impregnate herself with, say, Guy Sebastian's semen (the example they used). I think commercial radio was changing too. On certain stations it became all about shocking the audience, and sometimes humiliating them. I'm very relaxed about doing that to myself (the more perceptive among you may have gathered that), but no-one in our team wanted to do that to our listeners.

Having said all that, I also have to admit that I was just a bit crap at my job. Radio is a great medium, but I don't have the sort of skills you require for commercial breakfast radio. And weirdly what I wasn't good at was revealing stuff about my life. I'm fine at telling stories like the male prostitute one, or talking about death or adoption, but breakfast radio is all about sharing the minutiae of your life, and I've never been great at turning a story about making my own bread into spun gold. Partly, that could be because I don't cook, and it probably wasn't helped by not having kids, pets, hobbies or skills. So, while talking with the listeners was the highlight of the job for me, I didn't manage the intimacy that really great announcers have with their audience. I was also lousy at dealing with management and wasn't great in the face of adversity. Kaz and Pete were still based in Melbourne, so I was often alone in the studio and generally felt pretty isolated. Without Collin and Emma to talk to, I probably would have started going to work dressed in a camel costume. Actually, maybe that wouldn't have been a bad idea. That way, I would have had something to throw up in on the most nerve-wracking day of the month: ratings day.

After an almost inexplicable increase in ratings when we first started, it went from bad to worse. I was constantly in fear of losing my job. The anxiety I was experiencing ultimately meant that I was forced to have a colonic irrigation. For those of you who haven't had the experience, it's not a silent process and, as I lay there on the weird bed/toilet, listening to classical music, I wondered if this was the sort of accompanying performance Mozart had dreamed of when penning his concerto. And no amount of music or dim lighting can distract you from the fact that you are having litres of water pumped into your anus to flush out your intestines. I couldn't believe what was coming out. I'm pretty sure that I saw a chop that I ate in July 1984.

A large part of the reason for my arse troubles was that the show was doing badly and I was being paid a ridiculous amount of money. All talk of money makes me uncomfortable and, like directions, I simply retain nothing. I tried talking to a financial adviser. How I pitied this lovely woman, who may as well have spoken to me in musical notes or colours. She once asked me if I was all right and I had to say that the odd look on my face was a result of simply trying to listen to what she was saying without my mind going somewhere far away, anywhere – reciting Hall & Oates' lyrics would be preferable. Don't get me wrong, I like having money. I just don't like to think about it or deal with it in any way. I think this is probably because it was one of my parents' favourite topics before they came close to killing each other.

Boy, did I have money when I was on the wireless. I'd never before been paid the kind of money I was given to do breakfast radio, and no doubt I never will again. Collin and I lived in the nicest flat I've ever lived in, we ate in the nicest restaurants I've ever eaten in, we had a cleaner and we went on great holidays – you just know what's coming, don't you? I have, professionally and, to an extent, personally, never been more miserable. As well as being in a deeply unpleasant place to work, I was exhausted to the point of hysteria – radio dosh certainly didn't buy me happiness. I'm sure many an onlooker thought that they saw my relationship break up in restaurant after restaurant, whereas I'd probably just said, 'This is great polenta,' before breaking into uncontrollable sobs due to fatigue and stress.

I'm not saying I envied the poor. I didn't sit around drinking another expensive bottle of wine thinking, 'If only I was starving and had a child or two dying of malaria, then I'd really be living!' Nice stuff is great, but the money didn't make up for the fact that I was also completely disconnected from my friends because of the ridiculous hours that I was working. Because Collin was the one person I did see, it took its toll on our relationship too.

One of the other aspects of the job that didn't sit well with me was the obsession with celebrity. We interviewed a lot of very famous people and I'm telling you that Renée Zellweger doesn't have more to say than Jenny from Penrith, who called in to tell us a story so that she could win an Anastasia CD.

Towards the end of the first year, I had to fly to Palm Springs on a junket for *Ocean's Twelve*. Not a great movie, as most people who've seen it will tell you. I was so out of my mind by that stage that I thought it was a masterpiece (although that same year I bawled my eyes out at a film starring The Rock).

I'd never been around that many famous people before: Catherine Zeta-Jones, Brad Pitt, George Clooney and Matt Damon, to name a few. When I say 'around', I mean that I was at the press conference they gave and I got to do five-minute interviews with them in groups.

I found everything about it obscene. From the moment the producer kicked off the press conference, by telling us that he'd had to build the stars their own bar in Rome so that they could drink somewhere in peace, to Catherine Zeta-Jones assuring the women of the press that she often asked her husband Michael if her 'bum looks big in this', it was simply an offensive confirmation of how these people are treated because they're good-looking and okay at acting out other people's lines. I'm not saying that it's their fault (even if some of them clearly pursue the constant publicity they supposedly despise), and I think it would be dreadful to be that recognisable, but it really was as if the gods had stepped down from Olympus for a couple of days. The security made you think that we were at the White House, and it was difficult to miss the general contempt that anyone who had not been on the cover of *New Idea* was treated with. At one point a group of us had to vacate a room simply so Ms Zeta-Jones could walk from one side of it to the other. Was our mediocrity contagious? I did enjoy telling this story to my chiropractor's receptionist, who replied, 'I would've just said, "Get fucked, I'm an Australian."' I would have done if I hadn't been concerned that they'd shoot me.

These people had very little to say, yet here we were hanging off their every word. I knew that I would've had more fun talking to the catering staff. And good Lord, if I thought I was overpaid to do my job, how do you justify being paid millions of dollars to be in even a great movie, let alone a turkey?

I had to read all the celebrity magazines when I was on the radio, so I knew what was going on in these people's lives, and I cannot tell you how much I haven't missed reading that mindless garbage week in and week out. I don't care who Jennifer

Aniston is sleeping with. I'd certainly come a long way from the girl who dreamt of *being* one of these people. A lifestyle that I once fantasised would make me happy now struck me as being close to a criminal offence.

This was also the second time in my career (the first being when I started on television) that I noticed a marked jump in my own level of fame, in Sydney anyway. The most populated and glamorous city in Australia does seem a little preoccupied with the notion of celebrity, and my job meant that I was now mentioned in gossip columns and photographed at the few openings I attended. This was all about as pleasant as a trip to the gynaecologist to me. It hasn't happened very often, but having my picture taken while walking up a red carpet just makes me feel incredibly self-conscious and . . . I think the phrase I'm looking for is 'like a complete dick'. Apart from maybe Nicole Kidman, I'm sure a lot of people feel like that. I knew it was all part of the job but when I made it into the real-estate section of the paper (poor ratings must be the reason I was 'only renting'), I thought, 'If I'd given birth to a pygmy elephant, then maybe it would be worth writing about, but does anyone really care what a comedian on the verge of losing her job is doing?'

I read an article about an ex-contestant from some reality show who said that he loved his brush with fame because he never had to buy any drinks and got to sign a lot of women's breasts (even if he was also beaten up at least once). Maybe if I'd been offered the odd scrotum to autograph it would've been a different story, but the little fame I experienced wasn't for me.

I'm still embarrassed about the one time in my life that I actually used the phrase 'Don't you know who I am?' I was twenty-five, so it was when I was on *The Late Show*. I'd gone out to dinner with two friends and we'd all had a lot to drink. Unfortunately, two of us went to the toilet at the same time: one of us to violently throw up, the other to pass out. We were both gone for a while. By the time we got back, our friend Gill was in tears because she'd been harassed by a table of men in our absence. She'd complained to the management, but they hadn't moved her or done anything about it. That's when that awful line came out of my mouth. Of course, the manager didn't know who I was, and that's the assumption I've worked on ever since. Recently, a security guard asked me if I was still teaching at Wodonga TAFE.

Wouldn't it be great if you got a free drink not because you'd been on the telly, but because someone heard you'd had a lousy day, or that you were a nice person? Fame is such a ridiculous thing to put any stock in. It lasts for so few people. Do you remember what Skeet Ulrich looks like?

At least if you wind up becoming well known because you're good at something (hopefully not killing people), then it doesn't matter if the recognition lasts. Hopefully, you'll still enjoy writing, getting up at a comedy club, being involved with sport, or cooking, when the cameras aren't on you. What I don't understand is wanting to be famous for the sake of it. Is it so that you're remembered after you're dead? How's that going to help? Is being recognised, or even adored by strangers really going to fill any kind of hole? I was once at a concert where an audience member yelled out that they loved the singer, who replied, 'But you don't even know me.'

I understand that the wonderful thing about being a fan is that you feel that you know the person, to an extent, through their work. And, of course, you can feel that you would get on tremendously. I remember when I went and saw Bob Dylan, my friend Sue said, 'If only he knew what a great time he'd have if he came out with us all after the show.' We all agreed, but I don't know if that's true, because we were all very stoned. In fact, when we'd been parking the car, Sue had pointed to a Commodore and said, 'See, we need to find a park like that.' The car was indeed very close to the venue – but it was also crashed into a tree.

When I saw Liza Minnelli and someone yelled out their love, she replied whole-heartedly that she loved us too, and I believed her. I do love Liza, damn it, but on the question of fame being the answer? Well, your Honour, I rest my case. Then again, maybe I'm over-thinking all of this and people just want to be famous because they really like free shit.

Not that I had time for this sort of philosophising as I crawled towards the end of the year on the radio, with our ratings going from bad to worse. Straight after Palm Springs, towards the very end of the year, our little team did a week of shows at the Gold

Coast with some lucky listeners who'd won the opportunity to come with us. I say lucky because we all got to stay in the same hotel, which was called The Luxurious . . . Resort. All I can say is that whoever named that hotel must have at some point used the sentence, 'My, what a luxurious minimum security prison this is.' The building was next to a fun park, so you often heard the noise of children on the rollercoaster. One day, as a group of us were walking into the foyer, someone asked, 'What's that screaming?' Our producer, Emma, replied, 'It must be someone seeing their room for the first time.' Our group morale can be summed up by the very long lunch we had on the last day: someone made an inappropriate pass at someone, another person threw up, yet another started crying hysterically, someone passed out, two people nearly got into a fight and I did a headstand. Really. (I was actually all the other people as well.)

And then they offered us the chance to move back to Melbourne and take over the national drive-time slot. This was a demotion: Sydney breakfast is considered 'the jewel in the crown' (i.e., it's where all the money is). But I think the decision took us about fifteen seconds. For a stand-up comedian, being on a national show is much more helpful when it comes to touring, and the idea of being able to go to bed later than a nine-year-old and get up later than a rooster was way too appealing.

Life was looking up on drive: our ratings were slowly improving, and compared to what we'd been getting on breakfast, they were sensational. Our program director told us he was happy with the show and it actually crossed my mind, for the first time, that maybe when my two-year contract was up I could stand to do another year, because I wasn't suicidal anymore. That was a decision I never had to make.

I knew as soon as Collin told me that my manager, Kev, was dropping around mid-week for a chat. I opened the door and there he was, clutching a bottle of wine in each hand. 'How bad is it?' I asked. 'Are they just sacking me or the whole show?' He replied that it 'couldn't be more cunty': they were sacking me and Kaz, and keeping Pete (who apparently made the comment, 'Wasn't I good enough to be sacked?' God bless him).

Despite knowing that I was in no way cut out for commercial radio, especially breakfast, I was devastated. This was a lot worse than losing the napery job. Most of us have been sacked at some stage of our lives and it's simply a horrible feeling. A lot of comedians make the jump to commercial radio and have very successful careers, and I know that Kev had thought it would be the start of a long and lucrative one for me. I knew that wouldn't be the case on about day four, but still I would've liked to have left on my own terms. It was just humiliating and I toyed with the idea of never leaving the house again. Or having a face transplant. The truth is, nobody cared. I was walking down the street a good two months later and someone yelled out: 'I love you on the radio!' They hadn't even noticed.

*

The radio didn't quite have the health benefits I'd hoped it might, either. I did find a good yoga teacher but struggled to do it even once a week. Any sort of exercise would have been a tremendous help with my sleepless nights and stress. I was right about the hours making weeknight drinking pretty impossible, but they made sedatives and marijuana essential, and it would be fair to say that, overall, my consumption remained roughly the same. When I could, I would start drinking at about 9.05 a.m. on Friday, and would be pretty much drunk until early Sunday evening, when I would have to sober up and face the panic of returning to work on Monday.

So, all up – especially when you consider the fact that, along with the aftermath, I'd had a tube stuck up my rectum – the radio didn't really boost my health. I probably don't have to tell you that I didn't deal well with being sacked. Let's just say that in the routine I wound up writing about the whole episode, I liked to say that I drank myself a new arsehole. Mainly so that next time I had a colonic, I could have twice the fun. I did this for about three months – and then I actually had an epiphany.

Eventually it dawned on me, at the age of thirty-seven, that I'd been as much of a numbskull as Lucy Jordan, just in a different way. What was I DOING letting my job affect me so much? Everyone has good days and bad days at work, lucky breaks and unlucky ones. You encounter difficult people, you're sometimes laid off unfairly, and while it would be crazy to think that this was not going to influence your mental state, I was even crazier for letting it entirely dominate mine for years. Like my school results, success was always quickly forgotten, but any kind of failure or criticism was as tricky to get rid of as a stubborn case of crabs (I would imagine).

This really was the first time that I had failed spectacularly at something work-related. I mean, sure, I'd had bad reviews and shocking gigs, but nothing like this. It absolutely made me recognise that yoking my self-esteem entirely to my career was just nonsense. What I was tying myself to was other people's opinion of me, and working this out was a step towards wanting to make some kind of show about spirituality (something I would wind up being genuinely interested in), even if people thought I was crazy. It was great to finally have this realisation and there were a lot more to come. One of the most difficult was waking up to the fact that Prince Charming may have had a horse, but he didn't have the answer.

8

MORE BOYS

Despite the fact that I was just plain nuts after my father died, I did have the good sense to start dating a great guy – Gareth. I had at last hit on the idea that maybe alcoholic womanisers were not the way to go. (No offence, Dad.) Actually, I had nothing to do with it – Gareth pursued me and I was such a mess that I probably would have dated Mel Gibson if he'd asked me out. When Gareth initially showed some interest, I wanted to run a mile, until a friend said, 'He's really nice. Why don't you actually try going out with someone who will treat you well for a change?' Genius!

I shouldn't have been dating anyone, but what better distraction from grief than a relationship? And here was a decent, smart, talented musician, with terrific friends, who was fun and really liked me. And Gareth had lost his father some years before, so he knew what I was dealing with.

We'd been going out for a few months, when one day I came home to find a wall in my art deco flat had been removed. The real-estate agent had casually mentioned that the old building needed some work, and that this was going to happen, but I didn't expect to find a sheet of clear plastic instead of bricks at one end of my kitchen and bathroom, replacing an exterior wall. It was ludicrous. I couldn't offer the builders a cup of tea, but at least when I was showering they got to see my vagina. The plastic was replaced with plywood after a day or two and my whole flat was filled with dust to the point where a dune buggy would not have looked out of place. Naturally, when Gareth suggested I move in with him, it seemed like a good idea, especially when friends said, 'What's the worst that could happen? You just move out.' It's never that simple, and there is no way I should have landed my grief and insanity on this gentleman 24/7.

When Mum died not much longer after we'd shacked up, Gareth came to Perth with me for the funeral and did everything he could, because he's top-shelf. But grief can be pretty selfish too, and all I was interested in was drinking with my brother. That behaviour continued after we returned to Melbourne. I fell asleep on the couch with a glass in my hand far more often than I did beside him – they should put that position in the Karma Sutra.

It's something of a miracle my relationship with the lovely Gareth lasted as long as it did. But after nineteen months of this, one night we went to see the Coen brothers' movie *The Man Who Wasn't There*, after which we had a discussion where we both concluded that he shouldn't be either. I was no country for young or old men. This was my first lesson in realising that sometimes it doesn't matter how loving and supportive your partner is, they can't fix you.

Twelve months after Gareth and I broke up, I thought I'd pulled myself together somewhat. I had a fun weekly afternoon radio job, I was getting lots of other work, and thanks to both Jan's insistence and financial help, I'd just bought a little flat. My buddy Kaz came over and said, 'I guess all you need now is a boyfriend.' I replied that I really didn't want one. And I meant it. I wanted to settle into my apartment and just spend some time on my own, which is why, six weeks later, I had a boyfriend. In fact, I thought I'd found the man I was going to spend the rest of my life with.

I met Collin doing 'drunk yoga' in a beer garden. That's right – I was doing some yoga poses, pissed in a pub. I think it's fair to say that enlightenment was still some way off. A group of us went back to a friend's place. Neither Collin nor I have any recollection of having had a conversation before this interchange but I like to think that we did.

Me: 'Are you single?'

Collin: 'Yes.'

I then pushed him into a bedroom and we started to kiss. Would you have let a little lady like that slip through your fingers? I was sold when he came around to my flat not long after that, put my new bed together, made me dinner and then made wild passionate love to me. (If any gentlemen are reading this book, THAT'S WHAT WE ALL WANT.)

Collin is fascinating. He managed to grow up in Ireland without any kind of religion, but he certainly believes in – oh God, I'm really going to use this word – 'energy'. (Why can't there be fun words to describe this stuff? Like 'Winnebago'.) He's an artist and often goes on walks, which seem to me more like meditations. He really notices everything around him when he's outside and I will be forever grateful that I now look at the world a little differently when I'm travelling from A to B. I might pay attention to a flower or a cloud, which I never would have done before. I'm no Wordsworth, but it's sometimes nice to have a break in the endless stream of 'No really, let's think some more about me'.

Collin liked to talk about life, the universe and everything, and because I loved him, I'd listen. I didn't have any belief system myself, but because of my parents' death I was interested to hear how someone else was at least trying to make sense of it all. He didn't have any fixed views either, but he was a lot more curious than me. Sweet Jesus, we even watched *What the Bleep Do We Know!?* If you ever sit through it, I'd recommend that you fast-forward through the 'story' that involves the actor Marlee Matlin. Marlee's deaf and I'm afraid her performance made me wish I was blind. But some of the interviews are interesting, as people discuss everything from organised religion to quantum physics. Admittedly, I read an article in which a bunch of physicists said that all the people in the movie are crackpots, and you discover at the end of the documentary that one of the more charismatic speakers is apparently channelling an alien (that Star Trek outfit really should have tipped me off). Still, I enjoyed the conversations it inspired in Collin and I (though I should mention that we were often off our trees).

On Collin's and my first anniversary together, Kaz dropped me home and actually said, 'You don't think he's going to pop the question, do you?' I looked at her as if she'd just said that there was absolutely nothing irritating about Keira Knightley, and told her not to be ridiculous. Moments later, I was in my living room following Collin's instruction to look into the kitchen. When I turned around he was on one knee, and said, 'Judith Lucy, will you marry me?' I felt that the 'Lucy' part was unnecessary, unless Judith Durham was hiding around the corner and he was tossing up between the two of us, but I was stunned. Of course, I said yes.

I'd been vehemently against marriage until my brother's wedding, where everyone had such a good time (and I'd gotten lucky) that I realised it wasn't such a bad reason to throw a party. Even then, I hadn't thought it would happen to me. But here it was. People sent me engagement cards, the wonderful Lynda Gibson, knowing she wouldn't make it to the wedding, threw us a bridal shower, and Jan and I talked about dresses. I couldn't believe that I had found a fantastic, sweet, caring man to grow old with. At last, someone to 'complete me'.

All talk of weddings disappeared when I was working on breakfast radio. I saw more of Collin than anyone but still our lives felt dislocated. He dropped me at work every morning and listened to me unload about my bosses but despite his support, I felt quite alone in my distress. I now realise that cracks were starting to appear in the relationship, but I put all blame squarely at the foot of my job, and was convinced that once we moved back to Melbourne and I was working normal hours again, everything would be fine.

Collin then had to cope with my reaction to being sacked, and then with the bundle of nerves I was when I toured a one-woman show about my experience, called 'I Failed'. And I wasn't the only one experiencing some sort of crisis. Collin was going through his own shit, which I'm not going to go into here, but don't you love the way major relationship breakdowns often come to be symbolised by the trivial and mundane? Maybe one of you is having an affair or has a gambling problem, but you argue about cheese. We argued about a gate.

One day while I was at home someone walked through our pretty flimsy back gate and stole my bag and – this may not have made it into the police report – a pretty enormous pile of hooch. Collin swore he'd fix the gate and make it more secure. I don't know how often we talked about those few slats of wood and putting a proper lock on them, but it just never happened. Of course, it wasn't the gate that needed fixing, but a simpler solution seemed to be selling our flat.

There had been a couple of telltale signs that neither of us was making great decisions around this time. The first one was buying the expensive flat we'd previously been renting AFTER I'd lost my well-paid job. It didn't take us long to realise that we simply couldn't afford it, so we put it up for sale. I had to go to Perth for a couple of weeks during this process and Collin was so paranoid about messing the place up that he started living in the roof. He moved a mattress up there and that's where he slept. Moving house had turned my partner into Anne Frank.

We were both pretty paralysed during this period and I had certainly returned, yet again, to old habits. But that was okay, we could fix each other, couldn't we? That was what you did in relationships, wasn't it?

We tried counselling, we talked, we argued, I wrote him a letter trying to express everything. Nothing worked.

Collin is one of the nicest men I've ever met (a friend once said that she'd trust him to smuggle her child out of a war-torn country), but after close to five years, we called it quits. I can honestly say our relationship made me understand the truth behind that nauseating line that sometimes love just isn't enough.

A friend later told me that I'd been saying things like, 'No, Collin and I had a great lunch . . . I only cried once.' This would've seemed like a reasonable line to me, because for months the idea of us splitting was just inconceivable. I loved him and he loved me. He was a great guy and we were going to spend the rest of our lives together – I HAD THAT BOX TICKED. This was one area of my life that I did NOT have to worry about. So, it turned out that Mr Right wasn't the answer either – not if each person's opinion of themselves is as Mr and Mrs Wrong. Night after night, we'd sit in the living room with me pissed, stoned and watching television, and Collin stoned and on the internet – we'd be sitting less than a metre away, but I may as well have been on Jupiter. Both of us have subsequently made positive changes to our lives that we just weren't capable of when we were together. We couldn't help ourselves, or each other. I finally ended it and it remains the most difficult decision I've ever made.

I licked my wounds for about seven months. Thanks ultimately to buddies, and a better approach to work and yoga, I didn't entirely lose my shit but I was thirty-nine and a part of me became gripped with panic. Holy hell, was it now too late to find my soul mate?

My generation grew up with fairly confusing messages. I knew that, unlike my mother, I would have a career, but I also knew, like my mother, that I would spend most of my life with 'the one'. Why the fact that my parents argued every night hadn't alerted me to the fact that this whole idea was a crock, I can't tell you. But don't we all secretly think that the right person will be the answer, even if the evidence, right under our noses, seems to scream that it's simply not true?

Surely the reason most of us pursue anything – whether it's

money, Buddhism or a heroin addiction – is to fulfil some kind of longing. A feeling in our gut that something's not quite right with us, that there's something missing. A feeling that this surely can't be it. If it is, then why do we have this tinge of loneliness or melancholy? We're told that 'love' is the answer from a fairly young age, and while there are many different forms of that emotion, nothing makes you forget that slight feeling of emptiness more completely than falling wildly, dizzily, head over heels for someone. That wonderful/horrible, sickening/terrifying, all-consuming kind of love. I'm sure part of the appeal is that you actually stop thinking about yourself almost entirely. For once, you're only a bit player in the movie in your head, while the object of your affection is the star. What bliss!

I recently developed a totally unrequited crush on an actor I met who had starred in a local film. I'm so glad I didn't actually count the number of times I watched the trailer on my computer – let's just say I almost feel like I was in the movie. I'm forty-fucking-four. My behaviour is no different from the breathless excitement with which I used to greet an Adam and the Ants clip at fourteen. Age seems to have nothing to do with it. A friend's mum has just found love again in her seventies and she's apparently acting like she's a teenager again as well.

It's pretty difficult to ignore everything from fairytales to movies, from songs to advertisements, which tell us our soul mate is out there somewhere. I've cried my eyes out at everything from *The Way We Were* to *Notting Hill*. At least in the former they had the decency to show you that it doesn't always pan out. But it doesn't even seem to matter if I like the actors or the characters – not that long ago, I was crying to the point of nearly choking while watching *When Harry Met Sally*, for Christ's sake. I don't want to have sex with Billy Crystal or spend the rest of my life with his character, Harry Burns, who I find deeply irritating. I don't want to have what she's having, and how could I possibly relate to Meg Ryan when, especially these days, she looks like a cross between a mop and a duck? But these movies (and songs and books and paintings and magazine advertisements . . .) convince us that the answer lies not in ourselves but another person.

And there's no denying that this is particularly the case for the ladies. It has often been remarked that the two words 'bachelor' and 'spinster' have very different connotations. The former implies good times, freedom and being a man about town, whereas the latter condemns you to misery, loneliness and being found days after you've died, having had your face eaten off by your fifteen cats.

Not long ago, I attended the funeral of a man who had a very successful career but who'd been a big drinker with a string of relationships, many children and no real permanent address. He had very few possessions and was unequivocally viewed as being his own man and respected for it. I am one of the many who loved and admired him, but halfway through the service I was struck by the fact that if a woman had lived his life she would have been seen as tragic. No home, no permanent partner, not much of a mother to her many kids – what a sad old lush. A successful career, sure, but that won't keep you warm at night, will it? I don't know how many films I've see where if a woman puts her job ambitions first, she winds up bitter, an alcoholic or dead.

I recently said to an acquaintance that I envied her husband and family. To be honest, I knew she was feeling frustrated and bored because she was trapped at home with a newborn baby and, stupidly, I was trying to make her feel better. Talk about hoist by your own petard – when I quipped that that ship had certainly sailed for me (in terms of children, anyway), she said, 'I know, when I think of your life it makes me really sad.' I didn't know what to say. I had nowhere to go. I couldn't reply that I didn't want her life – which I don't – and I certainly wasn't going to agree with her. What brought me up short was realising that quite a lot of people probably think the same thing.

I don't want to be put in that box – and yet, I'm currently obsessed with the husband and wife in the teen drama *Friday Night Lights* (who have the best marriage in the world, and also happen to be fantastic parents), and frequently have to remind myself that it's a fucking TV show, and that I must stop crying because I'll never find a coach of a high-school gridiron team who will marry me and be an endless fountain of support, sexual desire, understanding, decency and humour, and who will occasionally, after a few drinks, knock a guy out for me. The part of me that isn't a complete lunatic knows that this is just manure, and yet I continued to chase it.

The first time I had sex after Collin was with an acrobat. Read it and weep, ladies. There weren't any swings involved, but I've never been with someone who was so physically relaxed. It's certainly the only time I've been in my bedroom and a man has turned to me and said, 'Do you remember if I brought my bag upstairs?' He said it in such a way that I thought he wanted his toothbrush or some deodorant, but he added: '. . . because I'm pretty sure I've got my cock ring on me.'

I remember thinking, 'Well, of course you've got your cock ring on you. Why wouldn't you have your cock ring on you? I mean, who goes out without their cock ring?'

Unfortunately, I confused great sex for intimacy. I finally worked out that I was barking up the wrong tree, when one night he asked if I had any action movies we could watch. I have nothing against them, but my Dolph Lundgren collection isn't as extensive as I'd like it to be. I hung in a bit longer for the sex, but stopped returning texts when I realised his shabby behaviour was never going to improve. I was only ever going to hear from him when he felt like it. He was careless rather than a bastard, and half the problem was probably that my desires were very different from his. And underlying it all was that he was only just about to turn forty and had no reason to worry – he wasn't about to become invisible.

After Mr Cock Ring, I went on a few dates with a very nice

man and managed to ignore some fairly loud alarm bells for a while, the most notable of which was his lack of interest. One night I actually launched myself at him while he was sitting on my couch. This wasn't easy, as he's tall and I'm pretty short. I was like a flea trying to leap onto the upper thigh of an uninterested Great Dane. A close friend finally pointed out that I was being a little desperate and I grudgingly had to admit that she was right.

And since then it really has been slim pickin's. Sometimes, it does feel like there was a big game of musical chairs in the mid to late nineties, during which most of my peers married or hooked up, and somehow when the music stopped I was left standing, with a Bacardi Breezer in one hand and a doobie in the other, saying, 'What happened? Who turned off the "Macarena"?'

And while I'm venting, why is it that men apparently peak in terms of physical attractiveness at the age when women are told they should start wearing a bag on their head? And how much more unfair is it that this is also when we're often at our horniest? I should really be grateful for that inflatable motorised couch with attachable vibrators that I took home the night I made a misguided bid at an auction for men living with HIV/AIDS.

I'm not sure when ageing came to be viewed as a disease. I've railed against surgery and cosmetic procedures for years, yet I understand why women feel pressure to look younger than their actual age, because that's the image of beauty we're surrounded by (even though a lot of people just wind up looking strange – a woman I know has injected so much stuff into her face and mouth that her head looks like a floatie with lips).

Grey hair doesn't bother me. I have a streak that makes me look a little Cruella de Vil, but I quite like that. My mother used to put a silver streak in one of her brown, curly wigs with a can of spray paint. Sure, people might hide their Dalmatians when I walk past, but I got that look going on for free!

I'd be lying to you if I said that I didn't want to get rid of the lines around my mouth, which make it look like I've slept face down on an egg slicer. Screw my lungs, no-one told me smoking was going to make me look like a monkey. Recently, I actually had an oxygen facial – I was paying for air. I love my beauty therapist and she offered to give me one for free. They pump oxygen into your pores with a tiny hose. It's meant to plump up your skin and feels a bit like a sleazy elf blowing on you for forty-five minutes. It would cost me well over two grand a year to keep this up and the only way anyone would notice is if I started dating Sherlock Holmes, or some other man with a magnifying glass. The really insane thing is that I generally like lines. I like being able to see someone's life in their face, but more and more you're left feeling that this is like saying you like anthrax. It's a pity that wisdom and maturity are so undervalued in our society.

Our insecurities about our looks are regularly confirmed too, because if a man our age does become available, he will often pair up with someone much younger. Tony Bennett met his wife when she was a foetus. I'm not making that up: her mother's a fan and was photographed with the singer when she was two months pregnant with Tony's current spouse. They started dating when she was eighteen and he was fifty-nine. I'd write Tony off as being too old for me, but the joke is that I'm WAY too old for him. I should have started dating middle-aged men when I was a zygote.

For the first time in my life, I think I now might know what I want out of a relationship and what I want in a man (a job, for example, would be great!), though the reality is that I'm forty-four and I have absolutely no guarantee that I'll ever meet that person. But what I've really learnt is that even if I wind up in my dream relationship, it's not going to solve my problems.

An acquaintance said to me recently that she didn't know what she would have done if she hadn't met her husband. He changed her life, gave her a reason to go on, and she would be completely at sea without him. I hope this doesn't come across as sour grapes, but what if he dies? What if he gets sick or falls in love with someone else, or simply out of love with her? Being in a good relationship can be great, but sometimes I wonder how often people are motivated by the fear of being alone and the idea that we need someone to fix us, or possibly to distract us by needing us to fix them.

It now seems ludicrous to me to think that you can find one person to satisfy all your needs. Like a lot of people, for a long time I believed it was possible, or even necessary, ignoring the fact that my friends had been giving me love, laughs and emotional support for years. Jesus, if only one of them would screw me, I wouldn't need anything!

9

FAMILY

It turned out that I still needed some fixing in an area in which I thought I was completely fine. When I broke up with Collin, I was in the middle of writing *The Lucy Family Alphabet*, a book about my parents.

You may have already gathered that Ann and Tony Lucy were fairly unusual people. Some of their peculiarities were cultural and generational, but that doesn't explain why my father wore makeup or why Mum told us that the shower was broken for fifteen years. It doesn't explain why my father's idea of a good time was blowing air up the family cat's arse, or why Mum would suggest that to clear my blocked nose I should inhale the termite-killing paint creosote, or why they neglected to tell me that I was adopted for twenty-five years. Not surprisingly, many of my early comedy routines revolved around these two pivotal figures.

My one-woman show about being sacked from the radio, 'I Failed', was one of the few pieces I'd done that made virtually no reference to Ann and Tony, although there was one punchline that involved me referring to Dad as being a 'bit of a cunt'. This prompted a birth cousin of mine to comment that I must have hated my adoptive parents, and *that* made me want to write a book about them, to set the record straight. I naively believed that was all that needed doing. I wanted to talk about my nutty parents as three-dimensional people. I wanted the book to be the full story and a full stop, and let's face it, I could really rip in because they were dead.

Writing the book is one of the best things that I've ever done. It was difficult to re-live some of my unusual childhood, but it was like doing therapy on speed. Even though my stand-up is personal, I don't think of it as being cathartic. I mean, sort your shit out before you share it with a bunch of strangers, would generally be my advice. I once saw someone talk about their family on stage and they burst into tears. Also, there were no jokes. Olivia was there that night, and she turned to me and said, 'I paid for a fucking babysitter to watch this?'

Because the process of writing the book was so immersive, it made me think about my childhood a lot more than I ever had. I'd done quite a bit of actual therapy and thought that I'd completely resolved all my issues with Mum and Dad, but the sadness and anger I felt while writing *The Lucy Family Alphabet* would indicate otherwise. I honestly feel that I came to know my parents better through the process of the writing, especially Mum. There's no denying that they were extremely wrapped up in each other and far from being the best parents in the world, but I came to understand their motivations a little better, and in the end I loved them more. I also believe that they gave it their best shot – as I think most parents probably do.

I remember finishing the first draft and thinking, 'Well, even if no-one buys this, I'm glad I did it.' Mainly it was because the process absolutely confirmed that my parents had truly loved me, and I them. I actually feel much closer to Ann and Tony Lucy now than I did when they were alive. Sure, it's lousy timing, but better late than never.

So, unresolved issues with your parents? Write a book! You might even make some cash out of it and get to hang out at writers' festivals. I loved this. People with nutty families would tell me their stories and elderly women with knitted berets would ask questions at the end of panel sessions, which they treated as excuses for them to talk about anything they felt like, including penguins. The point is, you sometimes don't know when you've truly resolved something deeply personal, and that not only is it impossible for it to be done for you by someone else, often you don't even seem to be able to control when you can do it for yourself.

An unexpected outcome from the book was that for about nine days it made me want to have kids. I woke up one morning feeling like that pop cartoon from the nineties, where a woman grips her head and says, 'Oh my God, I forgot to have children!' I'd always been dimly aware of the fact that my pathological

DRINK, SMOKE, PASS OUT

desire not to reproduce had been due to my upbringing, and the feeling that maybe offspring hadn't really been a fulfilling experience for my parents. After *The Lucy Family Alphabet*, I wondered if, had I dealt with some of this stuff earlier, I might have thought about having a family. I'm not one of those ladies who feels, to paraphrase a friend of mine, that I haven't climbed the mountain of womanhood by not having a baby (that just made me want to say, 'Listen, I've had a pap smear and as far as I'm concerned that's some pretty decent indoor rock climbing'). But it was interesting to think about how my life might have been different, and it gave me an insight, to some extent, into the sadness some of my friends feel because they haven't wound up having kids.

Jan always thought that she would marry and have five children but she's had to content herself with me. And I certainly feel lucky to have met her. In fact, during the first years of our relationship, I threw myself at her. I was angry at Mum and Dad for not telling me that I was adopted, and more generally just for being them. I couldn't get enough of this kind, intelligent, generous, sensible, NORMAL woman Jan, and we almost always have a lovely time when we're together.

This may have been stretched to the limit when we went to Italy. I would never have spent three weeks on a holiday with my adoptive mother – considering the only time the Lucy family went away we slept in our car, she would have been a little outside her comfort zone in a hotel in another country.

We had some good times, but it was certainly a mistake sharing a room. We might have gotten to know each other just a little too well. The two single beds were often so close together that sometimes I'd wake up in the night, see Jan beside me and think that I'd taken part in some sort of lesbian geriatric romp. And can you believe that I took a packet of condoms on this trip? What did I think I'd do with Jan if I met someone? Lock her in the wardrobe, or try and get her involved in a threesome?

Towards the end of the trip we were both tired, Jan was very ill, relations were a little strained, and then Paul Newman died. The star had been Ann Lucy's unabashed favourite, and suddenly he was on the cover of every magazine, and it was like Ann was shouting at me from the grave, 'Okay, maybe we only travelled as far as Albany and never got out of the P76, but don't forget about me!' And I didn't. There was even a note from the editor accompanying one of the Newman tributes, which described the writer's relationship with his mother. It talked of what an anxious person she'd been, but how she'd buried herself in movies and this was something they'd shared. I could have written that piece. On the flight home, I watched Mum's favourite film, *Lawrence of Arabia*, thought of her and wept like a baby.

And not long after I got back I had an experience where Mum really did come back and talk to me. About seven years after she died, I came upon a bunch of old photos and amongst them was a letter she had written to me two weeks before her death. I had absolutely no memory of it and can only assume that I read it once, was overwhelmed and so put it away for a time when I might be more up to reading it (and also hopefully sober). I may not have been there when my mother died, but she certainly did say goodbye. The letter says everything that I wish she'd been able to say to me while she was still alive. It is one of the few things I treasure. Now if only I could find one from Dad, the old cunt.

I love Jan, but I absolutely love my parents, who I think were largely responsible for how I turned out. And there was something about accepting who *they* were that finally made me accept who *I* was a little more, and realise that it could be a helluva lot worse. It finally made me let go of old story lines, embrace the cards I've been dealt, and just get on with it.

10

CITY OF CHURCHES

If there's a destination in Australia that comedians most take the piss out of, it's Adelaide, but I'm not one to poke fun at the city of weird murders, because for some reason it's the place where I've had a couple of experiences that helped me sort some shit out. It's kind of annoying that I couldn't have had these shifts in perspective in Jerusalem or Vatican City – even just for the frequent flyer points – but no, these little steps happened in the City of (oh, I get it now) Churches.

So, I like yoga. Not everyone does, nor even knows what it really is. There have been times when I've suggested to some-one that they try it and they've looked at me as if they think it involves pretending to be Yogi Bear for an hour. Whenever I went off to do a yoga practice, one of my partners would say, 'Oh, you're off for a snooze.' I also remember being asked by a surgeon, moments before going in for an operation to remove my gall bladder, if I did any exercise, and when I replied that I did yoga, he literally laughed in my face. It was as if I'd said,

'I find I get a really great workout from applying my deodorant in the morning – well, it *is* Rexona Sport.' People who don't
do yoga sometimes think that either it requires no effort at all
or that it involves behaving like the rubber man from a 1930s
freak show.

Even after I'd been doing yoga for some time, I still didn't
know everything it could involve. When I started, I liked the
physical aspect (hangovers permitting), and only through
reading the odd book did I become aware that there was a philosophy behind it too. While I knew that yoga could lead to
meditation, and that there was more to it than a gym workout,
I expected it to open me up to an interest in spirituality about as
much as someone doing boxing might think that pursuit would
lead them to write haiku.

A notion that I kept coming across in my reading was that
'I' was more than just the thoughts in my mind. In the past, I
might have agreed, and, as evidence, pointed out my sweet rack.
But because I was starting to realise that my ideas about work
or love being the answer were misguided, maybe I had become
open to the idea that being completely taken in by the endless
cycle of negative thoughts in my head was a mistake too. And I
was dimly aware of the fact that worrying about my job or my
relationship had never helped, though I didn't think that there
was anything I could do about that. But, boy, was I open to the
idea that I could.

So reading about this was as if someone had said, 'Oh, we

meant to tell you earlier that those lumps of flesh on the end of your arms are hands and you can use them to pick stuff up and do all kinds of useful things.'

I'm pretty confident that most people don't go around thinking, 'I'm good-looking, smart and kind, I react perfectly in every social situation, and I can make the person whose lucky enough to wind up in the sack with me come simply by making a noise like a panther.' While I'm convinced that some people only have white noise between their ears, or that sound a heart monitor makes when someone dies, aren't most us of just racked with thoughts of self-loathing, which manifest either as self-criticism or disparaging thoughts about life and others? (If I'm on my own here, I'm so screwed.)

When I read about the self being more than just your thoughts, I wondered what my idea was of what comprised 'me'. I suppose it had always been my body and what went on in my head. It had never occurred to me that my self-identity could be anything else, or that my thoughts might not be the truth. Obviously, I knew that when I'd fantasised about stabbing Sister Aileen in the chest as a teenager, it wasn't what I really wanted to do (probably), but I certainly believed that all my fears and anxieties, and fairly awful ideas about myself, were largely real. And they seemed to get more airtime than my hopes, fantasies or trying to remember where else I'd seen that actor playing the paedophile in this week's episode of *Law & Order: SVU*.

It had been in Adelaide where a friend had suggested my

trying yoga in the first place, and that city did it again during another tour in 2002. Gareth and I had parted at this stage and I was pretty much homeless, but travelling so much that it didn't really matter.

While I'd been doing yoga for a couple of years, I'd never bought a book about it that wasn't primarily about the poses, but in a bookstore in the City of Churches I came across *Living Your Yoga: Finding the Spiritual in Everyday Life*. It's a practical guide to incorporating yoga philosophy into day-to-day living, and includes mantras such as, 'The rowboat is empty' and 'Sell the goat'. Once, I would have said that these lines were about as useful as 'The tractor is shiny' or 'Bury the fish', but I read the explanations and tried to relate them to my life and experience of yoga. And they kind of made sense.

This was the moment I started to realise that the part of yoga I'd been doing drunk in pubs – the physical stuff – was actually not what it was about at all, or at least that you could choose to find much more in it. The ancient texts behind it offer a way to live your life that involves more than doing 'down face dog' shitfaced in a beer garden. This book takes some deceptively simple lines from one of those texts, explains them and then tries to put them in a modern context. A lot of it rang true for me but the chapter that really blew me away – and strap yourself in, because I'm going to sound like I have the IQ of a dried apricot – was about faith.

As a child, I was constantly being told that faith was something over which I had no control, but which I needed in order to believe in God. It was a 'gift' that had to be bestowed by the magical being I paradoxically struggled to have faith in. This yoga book said that faith is not about believing in something external or unknowable, but about believing in something within you. WHAT? This wasn't about slaying my only son, but about trying to believe in the part of 'me' beyond the flyblown chop that is my mind.

It's probably obvious that I'm trying to avoid words like 'soul' and 'essence', and even 'consciousness', because they can be off-putting. But while the words can make me uneasy, it did somehow make sense to me that we are more than our bodies and mind, and to be perfectly honest, I didn't care that I didn't entirely 'get it'. It was the first time I had entertained these possibilities, and all I knew was that I was starting to feel a lot better.

This is a little mortifying, but when I returned to Melbourne this idea prompted me to hang out a lot in the spiritual sections of bookstores. I started reading everything from *Conversations with God* to *Finding your Northern Star* (for the life of me, I can't remember what the hell that one was about). I didn't lose my mind, though. Some of the stuff I read was interesting and occasionally struck a chord but a lot of it made me angry, too. *Conversations with God* made me particularly cross. I recall a passage towards the end where the author made it clear that God was talking so damn much to him, he was just going to have to write another book. So I guess God's wise, He's just not very succinct. I'm sorry, but this guy may as well have written: 'I haven't made enough money out of this patronising pile of crap, so I'm just going to have to keep churning them out. Stay tuned for *Conversations with God 3, 4* and *5*. Possibly followed by *Conversations with My Own Arse: A True Journey of Self-discovery*.'

Adelaide wasn't done with me, though. The same friend who'd advised me to get a yoga teacher had a massage appointment she couldn't make, and offered me her spot. I love a massage – sometimes it's the only physical contact I'll receive in months. And my friend told me that this masseur was so popular she couldn't bear her booking going to waste. It was a type of massage called kahuna, originally from Hawaii. I knew nothing about it but when she told me that a session generally lasts for two hours or more, I became very excited.

About ten minutes before I was going to call a cab, she rang to tell me that nothing about this experience was going to be like any other massage I'd had. The masseur, Frank, operated in a room in his house, in the middle of nowhere, I would have to get completely naked and he looked a little like an extra from *Goodfellas*.

This was all good to know, because it all turned out to be true – had I not been prepared, I'm pretty sure I would have run from the room screaming when he started covering my body in copious amounts of oil, as we listened to the first track on his very eclectic music tape, which happened to be Ravel's 'Bolero'.

(I still associate this piece with the Dudley Moore film *Ten*, so if my friend hadn't pre-warned me, I might have assumed I was in for a very greasy sexual assault.)

Kahuna's an unusual technique: your modesty is preserved with a sheet as you're repeatedly stroked rhythmically in time with the breath of the practitioner. I lay there thinking that this approach was interesting, just not particularly effective, but then, after all the vacuum cleaner–like breathing, he suddenly concentrated on my problem areas, the places where tension had turned parts of my body to rock, and he released them like they had never been released before. My muscles just turned into custard. It was the result of the longest foreplay I'd ever experienced.

Frank had told me that some people get very emotional at the end of the process, but I was sure that this wouldn't apply to me. I don't generally like to let my guard down in front of strangers (unless I've had a few wines on a plane – then I can cry hysterically at anything from the news to a bad Jack Black comedy). At the very end of the massage, he covered me completely with a sheet, like a cheap parent trying to help their kid out with a ghost costume, and simply held me. You don't have to be Uri Geller to guess my reaction – it was like watching *Year One* all over again. It was a truly amazing experience and the first time I'd ever met someone who I would honestly call 'a healer'. When I say that, I mean someone who genuinely wants to help others simply for the sake of helping others. There's a fee, but it's pretty small, and Frank oozes a kind of empathy that

I sometimes feel you could only possess because at one time you needed it yourself.

Frank is an extremely shy and unassuming man who also happens to raise and slaughter cattle. A very difficult life led him to this kind of massage and I'm unsurprised that, without any advertising, he is constantly booked out. I like to think that I have a fairly strong bullshit meter and I believe that the only kind you'll find around Frank will be the real stuff on the soles of his boots. I see him every time I'm in Adelaide and feel very lucky to have met him. I don't know exactly what he believes, but the room he practises in has a picture of the Virgin Mary on the wall as well as iconography from other religions. I'm fairly certain that he doesn't subscribe to a particular faith, but he obviously believes in something. Once he said to me, and he is a man of very few words, 'Remember, God, or whatever you want to call it, made you, he loves you and he wants you to be happy.' If anyone else had said this to me I would have thrown up on their shoes but somehow, coming from Frank, I found it strangely comforting.

My last Adelaide moment came at the very end of this same trip. I was on a mid-morning flight back to Melbourne and, thanks to the final night revelry of the Adelaide Fringe Festival, was a little worse for wear. Naturally, as soon as we were airborne I ordered a bloody mary. I was seated next to a particularly attractive middle-aged woman. She had a silver bob and wore a very stylish, tailored suit. As the flight attendant passed me my drink, she said, 'Boy, that looks good.' I remember thinking that I liked the cut of this woman's jib and that if I wasn't so hung-over I would probably enjoy chatting to her. I don't want to admit this, but I actually had a sense that I *should* talk to her – and yes, that could've been the vodka talking, but somehow we did, too.

She was great. She was funny and smart and I remember thinking that if I could be like her at that age I'd be pretty happy. Then, out of nowhere, she asked me if I'd ever taken a personality test and what did I think of Kirstie Alley? She actually asked me if I'd ever tried meditation and I told her that, while I was dabbling with yoga, and was certainly interested, it seemed a long way down the track. There is a lot about this conversation I don't remember, but I do recall her telling me that she used to be an incredible (in her words) 'party girl'. She said that she'd loved drinking and boys (I can't imagine why I'd taken a shine to her), but that, while she still enjoyed a wine, meditation had brought her a lot of happiness. She told me that initially she'd been terrified of the idea and was scared of what she'd find if she managed to be still and get beneath her thoughts. In the end, she said, 'What I found was love, nothing but a feeling of pure love.' Not only did I like this woman but I related to her, and it was the first time someone who wasn't stoned or a hippie had talked to me about this form of relaxation. It would be some time before I really committed to meditation, but another seed had been planted.

*

While Collin and I were still together, I started doing yoga with a lovely woman called Jen, who lived just around the corner from us. A sign in her front garden alerted me to her classes. I liked her, and the yoga incorporated some moves from a type called Shadow Yoga (I actually like to call it 'Shadow . . . shadow . . . shadow yoga' in an ever-decreasing whisper), which was quite challenging and I enjoyed that too. Gradually, I'd started reading fewer *Road Less Traveled*–type books (not that I actually read that one, or *The Secret* – in my opinion, that's what it should have remained, and there's a reason that road has remained less travelled), and I started reading more books on yoga philosophy, such as a translation of the sutras of Patanjali. I realise that will make as much sense to some of you as saying that I started reading some alien transcripts from the planet Zertong, but they're basically ancient teachings that are pretty much the backbone of yoga as we know it, and they deal with a lot of esoteric ideas in practical ways. The sutras are usually only a few words long, although, remarkably, they contain more wisdom than most of Ashton Kutcher's tweets. This guy Patanjali really did know how to jam some meaning into 140 characters.

I know that yoga has become nauseatingly fashionable. A few years back, someone asked me if I'd started doing it because of Madonna and Gwyneth Paltrow (which was just insulting – my only celebrity role model is Jennifer Lopez). I think one of the reasons it has become so pervasive is because it offers different things to different people – women especially. (Although, Jesus wept, when are single men going to realise that if they want to meet some ladies, they should go to a yoga class? Gentlemen, it's like fish in a barrel.) For some, it's simply a way to get fit or flexible, or even to lose weight. Other people do it to improve their breathing or to make a pregnancy easier. Still others just want an hour a week to themselves, where they can really relax. You don't have to learn any of the Sanskrit terms for the asanas, and you certainly don't have to read one word of the philosophy, although it seems to be quite a common experience to start off with just the physical interest and gradually become more involved. That was certainly what happened to me.

The point is that on a very basic level, at the initial stages, yoga was making me and my habits healthier and the philosophy was very gradually helping me to understand a little about how my mind worked. That seemed more effective than a flagon. Of course, I realise that some people achieve a kind of stillness or mental clarity through swimming, walking or even golf. Some people pray, my housemate believes cooking is like a meditation for her, and I think it's not always what you do, but your intention when you're doing it. Maybe I needed yoga because it so obviously offers itself up as something that can help you get your mental crap together. Mind you, the wonderful and venerable Robina Courtin, a Buddhist nun who we interviewed for the TV show *Judith Lucy's Spiritual Journey*, said she couldn't stand yoga and that the class she attended was simply a lot of people breathing up each other's bottoms.

But yoga gave me hope and made me realise that there was a way to deal with negative thoughts other than with shiraz. I still didn't know what I believed, if anything, but I became keenly interested in the idea of finding out. Several years ago, when I came up with the idea of writing this book, it was that optimism that inspired the idea. I felt better than I had in a long time and I thought that maybe sharing some of my experiences might help other cynics look at the whole spirituality thing in a way that didn't make them puke. So a yoga class led me to writing a book and doing my first television series, on goddamned spirituality.

Something I realised not long before making *Spiritual Journey* is that nothing about life is linear. It's like when a friend said to me, 'In the eighties, I thought feminism was heading in one direction; that stuff was just going to get better and better for women.' I don't want to shock anyone, but I don't think this has happened. I would go into why, but I'm just off to my pole-dancing class – one day, I hope to be as sassy as the Pussycat Dolls.

This pertains to any change, I think – in fact, if my experience is anything to go by, for most of us change is REALLY SLOW. And, to be frank, it's all pretty embarrassing how slow it was for me. It had taken me close to forty years to work out some stuff that amoebas probably already understood:

incredibly basic life lessons, like that the answer isn't at the bottom of a bottle; sometimes love isn't enough; work to live, don't live to work . . . Before long, it was going to dawn on me that too many cooks can spoil the broth and a bird in the hand is worth two in the bush. And what's even more humiliating than realising I should have paid more attention to the thoughts of the day on my grandmother's calendar is that despite these revelations, I was still a long way off from actually changing my behaviour.

I read somewhere that if you're going to commit to some sort of spiritual practice, then somewhere, even if it's very deeply buried, you like yourself enough to try and change a little for the better. I like to think that this was finally being reflected in some of my choices. Before starting to film the show, I was certainly 'better' in terms of my mental and physical health. The more you do yoga, the better it makes you feel, so gradually you learn to let go of bad habits. As a teacher once said to me, 'It's more as if smoking or drinking give you up – you're just not as interested anymore.' Smoking and drinking certainly weren't keen to give me up altogether (do those vices have no self-control?), but yoga was making me feel so good that it seemed more and more ridiculous to jeopardise a regular practice or going to a class by trashing myself. Yoga offered a very different kind of high, which didn't involve eating two pizzas and a jar of Nutella. I was also now attending a school that completely specialised in Shadow (shadow . . . shadow . . . shadow . . .) Yoga, which I was coming to love.

The need to concentrate on a pose frees your mind from all the stuff that generally bombards our heads. The exercise and concluding relaxation help with everything from sleep to anxiety. The practice and philosophy combined encourage you to worry less about your thoughts and be more aware of what is going on in the world around you.

And all that means that slowly you come to see yourself as not at the centre of things all the time. Admittedly, as a performer, I know that's not true. (I mean, come on, why wouldn't it be all about me? I'm fascinating.) But it really was a relief to get a break from that isolation we can all sometimes feel, and to know that while everyone has their own stuff going on, we're all in this together.

I remember a yoga class that brought this home. I wasn't well, so was forced to sit up the back and just watch my teacher, Louise, and the other students. While yoga might give you an inkling that the world doesn't revolve around you, sometimes in a class you can be oblivious to that because you're so immersed in what you're doing. This time, off the mat, it was fascinating to see how different everyone's experience was, although they were all doing roughly the same thing: there were people who I'd always assumed were far more flexible than me, struggling with certain poses that I found easy, but there were others who could do certain asanas that are near impossible for me, with an ease that I found surprising. Everyone in the class was different in ability, age, experience and approach, but united by the poses and the class itself, all muddling along, doing their best, and everyone with their own Achilles heel. Even though I hadn't wanted to admit it, I think a part of me had always been quite competitive when it came to yoga, and I suddenly realised how completely absurd that was. It didn't matter how 'good' any of us were at the poses, what mattered was that we were all here and all trying. Again, there are other ways to get to some perspective on your own existence. One, I would imagine, is becoming a parent – you're a part of something that has been happening as long as we've been around, and (generally speaking) you will die and your children will grow up, and so it continues. A yoga practitioner just does it with less toddler vomit on their T-shirt.

But despite certain lifestyle improvements, and talking like a cross between Deepak Chopra and a poster involving sunflowers, I was still behaving like a complete dickhead.

I was continuing to make some pretty bad life choices, as I think they're called, and overindulging without too much encouragement. This became apparent not long before I started work on *Spiritual Journey*, when I signed up to do a yoga intensive.

The course was to be taken by the founder of Shadow Yoga, Zhander Remete, a sixty-something Hungarian man who speaks a little like the Count from *Sesame Street* and who I'd first encountered by watching one of his DVDs, in which he wore nothing but a black leather thong. I'd bought his book some time beforehand but had been warned that I would understand little of it. That was actually an optimistic prediction: I was confused reading the contents page. But my teacher, Louise, is such an admirer of his, and I'm such an admirer of hers, that I was compelled to experience his teaching methods firsthand.

I'd been to a week of his classes about eighteen months earlier but had stood so far down the back that I may as well have been in another room. Zhander had an undeniable presence and dedication, but there was no denying that he was a little scary in how intense and committed he was. My feelings about him were probably best summed up by a complete stranger, who turned to me about halfway through the week, when we were putting our shoes on, and said, 'You know, half the time I think that this is amazing and he's just incredible, and the other half of the time I think that he's crazy and I have no fucking idea what I'm doing here.'

This time round, I was going to try and be pretty intense as well. The course was three weeks long. As well as the yoga, I was going to eat really well and not drink, at all, for the whole time – not a drop, not a shandy, not even cough mixture. The course was going to be a circuit-breaker, a long-overdue break, and also the moment to prove that my habits could change. I'd always believed I didn't need to drink every day, so what the hell, why not? As a consequence, I'd not gone without alcohol for so many days since I'd sat my final school exams . . . so, just the twenty-five years. Looking back, it's obvious that

I was building myself up for some sort of freak-out, and boy, did I have one.

About four days out from the beginning of the intensive course, I missed a class that would have been useful. I didn't think much of it and asked Louise if we could have a private lesson, something I did occasionally to make up for missing one. She sent an email back simply saying 'No.' I now realise that this was because she was going away the next day and replied to my email at two in the morning, along with a stack of others. But I reacted as if she'd actually written, 'I loathe you and I wish you and your entire family were dead.' I interpreted her abruptness as some sort of 'tough love' to prepare me for Zhander, and I decided I really didn't need this shit in my life. Here's what my mind told me: 'How dare she? She doesn't know what's going on with me – maybe I really couldn't make it to class [I could have]. What on earth am I getting myself into? I mean, if Louise's email makes me feel like this, what am I going to do if Zhander's critical of me? Isn't yoga meant to make me feel good? Don't I have enough things in my life that make me anxious and stressed?'

The fact that Louise obviously hated me made me go into a complete spiral about everything from my family to my career to being single, and why not freak out about the chunk of hair that had come out of my head that morning in the shower? I'm not on FUCKING CHEMO, WHAT'S HAPPENING TO ME? OLD, ALONE AND BALD – OH, GREAT.

FUCK YOGA.

So I booked a ticket to Perth (I was long overdue for a visit to see my birth mother and brother), drank heavily and sent my teacher a polite email saying that I didn't think I was ready for the intensive.

All of that from a one-word email. (I hope I'm making everyone feel a little better about their lives.)

I'd managed to take something important to me – albeit something that I knew would be a challenge – and turn it into a bad decision. I was utterly convinced that I'd done the right thing by cancelling. I knew that I would stick with yoga, but I'd already decided on another school that I would start attending, despite the fact that I didn't much like the style.

The day before the intensive, I got home from a long lunch only to discover that Louise had not only emailed me but called twice to tell me that I had completely misinterpreted her. The third time she rang, I picked up. She was so damn lovely that I wanted to weep. She'd worked out that I was completely terrified. She told me that the next morning she would save a space for me right next to her. Eventually, I agreed to come and felt like a complete idiot.

For the first few days, I really was terrified and concentrating so hard that it was a miracle I didn't spontaneously combust. By the end of each session, I was the colour of a fire truck – I looked like you could fry an egg on my face. This, combined with very unladylike perspiration, convinced me that the reason Zhander was being nice to me was because he was concerned he might have to call an ambulance and report a cardiac arrest.

Slowly, it became less like being a gymnast in Communist China training for the Olympics. It got easier and I actually got to the point where I almost looked forward to getting out of bed in the morning. And, in the end, it made me feel a lot fitter, saner and healthier, and surprisingly, going without alcohol wasn't difficult at all. There were times when I craved a single drink but that was about it, and that included my birthday. I went out and saw a band and caught myself thinking, 'Oh my God, it's possible to go out and have a good time without drinking! I won't be hung-over tomorrow and I'll remember the entire evening!' What a revelation to have at forty-one.

Ultimately, it confirmed for me that yoga is not really about the physical, it's about the mind; my biggest challenge hadn't been a pose, it had simply been committing to the intensive course and, therefore, change. But the classes also taught me about acceptance. You can't push a pose or your level of understanding. You can do or read something again and again and then suddenly it clicks, and those moments are fantastic, but if you force anything you're wasting your time. Accepting where you are seems to be everything. That doesn't mean you don't try, rather that you keep trying and accept that sometimes you won't succeed. It means that you're more alive to what's actually going on than what you wished or feared might be happening. You realise that resisting means you wind up missing what's happening to you right now.

Perhaps the highlight of the intensive, though, was when I overheard Zhander talking to a bunch of students about 'the eagles'. I thought this must be a metaphor or some obscure yoga reference. It turned out it was the 'Desperado' Eagles, and it made me laugh to think that this man I was initially so intimidated by was a fan of easy listening – he's probably got a soft spot for Toto.

11

TELEVISION

Before *The Lucy Family Alphabet* was released, the ABC contacted me to see if I'd be interested in developing a show about my childhood on the strength of a newspaper piece that I'd written about a family holiday. It turns out that trip to Albany was a great investment – the story was the first step to my doing a six-part TV series.

Initially, I jumped at the chance, but the further along the process went, the more I realised that the book had already said everything that I had to say about my parents and that doing a show about them would just feel like I was going backwards. When I thought about what I was really interested in doing a program about, the answer was spirituality (once I'd worked out that sucking tequila out of Ryan Gosling's navel wasn't a concept I could build a show around).

I'd been slowly realising which of the reasons to get out of bed in the morning didn't make sense to me anymore, and trying to replace them with reasons that did. I'd been pretty good at crossing stuff off my list but, outside of yoga and reading everything from *Eat, Pray, Love* to ancient and slightly mystifying texts like the Bhagavad Gita, I seemed to have little to add to the positive column. But I had at least figured out that pursuing work that meant something to me made a big difference. And now I was lucky enough to have the opportunity to make a TV series, and I could make it about something that mattered to me, and hopefully to others. Not only did I want to try and discover what on earth I believed in, I suddenly wanted to know what everyone else did too.

One of my oldest friends wound up telling me that she'd been deeply involved in kabbalah for years. I couldn't believe she hadn't told me before, but she said I'd never asked and that we simply never had conversations like that. How is it that I knew which of my friends had herpes but not what they thought being alive was all about? Not for the first time in my life, I felt like a complete idiot. I had really managed to ignore the fundamental questions, by getting off my face and watching a lot of cop shows.

Many years ago, I received a review that described any appeal I had as being that I was so *ordinary* (which was certainly better than the one that described me as 'simply awful' – no reading between the lines there). So, I figured that if an ordinary person like me was interested in this stuff, then so were a lot of other people, and maybe, like Elizabeth Gilbert, I'd wind up banging someone who looked a bit like Javier Bardem.

The idea for the TV show was to retrace my steps from Catholicism to atheism, to my current love of yoga, to who knows where. I'd talk to people about the fundamentals of life, experience their practices firsthand wherever possible, and throw in a few sketches and cheap gags along the way.

We spoke to nuns, a priest, an ex-priest, psychics, New Age healers, Aboriginal elders, Buddhists, atheists, a Hindu priest and, just to keep it personal, a few friends of mine along the way. What I found so impressive about almost everyone we encountered was that they had dedicated years, if not their entire lives, to trying to figure out what it was all about. With the exception of the female Aboriginal elders I spent time with, who were born into the spirituality that encompasses their existence, most of the interviewees had either walked away from an old life or rejected much about it to search for meaning. Very few of the men and women we spoke to had typical lives; they weren't interested in money and possessions, or even a family or partner, in many cases. They had embraced celibacy and given up careers, and one woman, Shivani, had left behind everything she knew in the States to worship Shiva in India. I'm not saying we should all be running around in loincloths, talking to dolphins or drinking our own urine, but it was inspiring to see the different choices these people had made. Jesus, all I'd been trying to do initially was to avoid having a liver transplant like Larry Hagman.

Making the show was just an absolute joy. I got to work

with a wonderful group of people and totally immerse myself in a world I found gripping. I'll share one sentence from the largely mortifying diary that I kept while we were shooting *Spiritual Journey*: 'I feel so privileged to be doing this.' In my notes I sound mostly like a cross between Dorothea from *Middlemarch* and a drunken Doctor Phil. But time and again, I was struck by people's candour and sincerity, whether I was talking to a Catholic priest or a bald guy called Darpan who did some Shamanic journeying with me. Even if you think that what a person believes is CRAZY (and believe me, there were actually times, generally when we were in Byron Bay, when I would find a person's belief system so ludicrous that I'd picture my father in his coffin to stop myself from laughing), if they seem decent and they have faith, it's difficult not to be touched by them.

And it really felt like people gave of themselves. Often it was just for a moment or two, but occasionally someone would make themselves so vulnerable, in such an honest way, that it was impossible not to return that openness. There were times when you could tell that someone's guard had dropped to such an extent that they even seemed to surprise themselves. I mean, sure, in the past I'd opened up about getting blind, kissing a gay man and throwing my underwear out the window, but this seemed a little deeper and again gave me a sense that we're all in this together.

On the practical experience side of things, I got to do everything from hanging out with nuns to attending a ten-day silent Vipassana meditation retreat. I spent nights camping in the desert just outside of Alice Springs with three amazing Aboriginal women, witnessed people speaking in tongues and did yoga on a boat in the Ganges. I was massaged, had tarot and astrology readings and was even re-birthed. I don't regret anything I tried, but the things that have stayed with me are the ones where I truly experienced a sense of peace, a sense of being completely present. By that I mean not thinking about anything else apart from what was happening, not even the fact that I was on camera making a TV series. One of the people we interviewed for the show (but who didn't appear in the end) was an ex-Jesuit priest, John Honner. At one point, off-camera, he said to me, 'You know what the secret is, don't you? Being still.' By the end of making the series, I had worked out that he wasn't referring to those wankers that cover themselves in paint and stand frozen in a mall, expecting you to give them money. (What for? How is not moving a skill?) And I also came to realise that many different things obviously work for many different people.

EPISODE 1: GENESIS

I must say that the faith of my childhood seemed to haunt the whole shoot. So many people we encountered, even if they are now a Buddhist nun or a shaman, had been brought up Catholic. It certainly does seem to be difficult to let go of entirely. Even the phrase 'lapsed Catholic' somehow sounds like a temporary accident. Like you'll wake up one morning and think, 'I don't believe in sex before marriage anymore – someone get me a Bible, a priest and rip this IUD out of me!'

I know people who are now atheists who have sent their children to Catholic schools, and apparently it's not hypocritical at all to get married in a lovely church even though you don't go to mass. I also know people who think it's all bullshit, yet they've baptised their children. My birth mother rarely goes to mass and never takes communion, but used to pop into a chapel at her work to say a prayer. And the people I know who aren't interested in keeping their options open when it comes to Catholicism, often seem to loathe it with such a passion that it's difficult not to think that they protesteth a bit too much.

I honestly believed for a long time that I had walked away from Catholicism relatively unscathed, yet a few years ago I became almost evangelical about a documentary called *Deliver Us from Evil*, a deeply disturbing look at the abuse that has occurred within the church. I wanted every Catholic, practising or lapsed, to see it. As well as the horror of the physical abuse, it captures the devastation families feel at having their faith taken from them. The glue that held their lives together was stripped by the priests who betrayed them and then the institution that protected the perpetrator and not the victim. It's not like having a family doctor exploit your trust – for these people, the man who betrayed them REPRESENTED GOD. They were truly shattered, and lost everything: community, trust and purpose. And maybe that's why those of us who weren't abused can still relate to this documentary, even to a small degree: the rug that was our way of explaining the world was pulled out from under us when we woke up to the shortcomings of the institution.

But why did I care so much? Why on earth did it bother me when people took photos in a church in Italy? The logical part of my brain said that I really shouldn't have been fussed if they'd been filming *Jesus Christ: Super Scrotum* in front of the altar. As you can tell, I had some pretty mixed feelings about the Church, so I was curious and a little anxious to see what taking a walk down my religious memory lane would do to me when we filmed material for the first episode of *Spiritual Journey*.

Something I was not expecting to be touched by was spending time with some Catholic nuns. One of the things my mother always loved to say, when she wasn't talking about joining the IRA, was that nuns have a great life. She'd see my primary school headmistress, Sister Florence, zipping around in a new car or off to a retreat in Europe, and jealously quip that she'd love that life (a lot of my mother's fantasies seemed to rely on not having children, which was difficult not to take just a little personally). I think she kind of forgot about the poverty vow and helping others. As far as Ann Lucy was concerned, these nuns were virtually Hugh Hefner, living the high life. I knew Mum's idea was completely off the mark, but I had no real clue what being a nun was like, and since it was the only 'career'

I'd ever really entertained, apart from being a performer, this seemed like a great opportunity to find out.

I don't know how seriously I thought about being a nun as a child. It's easy to think that marrying God is a great idea when you're twelve. I didn't know, at that age, that life might hold many temptations that I would at least like to try. At that point, my idea of a good time was a Warner Brothers cartoon and a mug of Milo. In truth, I let go of the idea pretty quickly, essentially because my big brother was scathing about it, but I would've jettisoned it anyway, once I'd realised that it was incompatible with a life on the stage and all of that blow I planned on taking with Robert Downey Jr.

Now, here I was at forty-two, single, childless, not much of a family – OH MY GOD, HAD I MADE THE WRONG CHOICE? When I requested of our show's incredible researcher, Robyn, that it would be great if we could find a nun my age so we could compare our lives, I wasn't really holding my breath. Even when I was at school the younger nuns all seemed like the walking dead (they were probably in their thirties). But, true to form, Robyn found Sister Rebecca McCabe, a Mercy sister only a year older than me, living in Sydney.

Rebecca is a physiotherapist in a health centre and a senior clinical researcher at Greenwich Hospital in Sydney. We met her at the clinic where she does physio and I liked her immediately. I don't know what I was expecting, but I wanted to say, 'But you're just so normal.' Maybe I thought she would be overly pious or lack a sense of humour, because of my dealings with nuns as a kid. Or maybe I thought that she would sound like Sister Gemma, a nun we had in primary school who'd had her voice box removed and looked a bit like Rod Steiger.

The next day I went to Rebecca's home. She lives in a villa, one of three each occupied by a nun, although Margaret and Pauline are considerably older. At first I was actually a little shocked. Where were the habits? Was Rebecca really wearing a denim jacket? Why don't they just put on some bikinis and high heels? As soon as I saw the lovely modern homes with their large-screen televisions, I thought of Mum. As I sat down with the women to enjoy lovely pasta and a glass of wine, I could just hear her saying, 'See I told you – they live great lives. What I wouldn't have done for that freedom.'

They do have independence to an extent now, but that's a relatively recent development, and it was saddening to hear the older nuns talk of a time when becoming a sister meant virtually leaving your family for good. They spoke of visiting the sick in hospital but of not being allowed to visit their own dying parents, and crying themselves to sleep at night.

Margaret and Pauline seem to have had no trouble embracing the modernisation of the Church. They said that convent life not only lacked privacy, but that friendships weren't encouraged because of a fear of homosexuality, even though, as Pauline put it, 'We didn't even really know what that was.' These remarkable women dedicated themselves to God at very young ages. I know they were growing up in a different time, but still, the idea of knowing that you wanted to be a nun at thirteen, as Pauline claims, seems incomprehensible to me. All I knew at that age was that I wanted to get my hands on the Loverboy single 'Turn Me Loose'. I was struck by how intelligent and warm these ladies are. How they love to engage in thoughtful conversation and have no problem being critical of the Catholic Church. They talked of its sexism and hypocrisy, and yet this is clearly all secondary to their love of God and their passion for social justice . . . oh, and sport. They don't have big tellies for nothing.

Rebecca has never worn a habit or lived in a convent, and admits that it might've been a different story if she'd had to do those things. She became a nun at twenty-five because she 'wanted to do something radical'. My idea of radical was getting an asymmetrical bob. She'd been a champion swimmer as a child, ninth in the world at one point, but when training for the 1984 Olympics she sustained a shoulder injury that was the beginning of the end of her career. She'd stopped attending mass at fifteen, but, as often seems to be the case, a major shift in her life made her question what the point of it all was.

This was the first of many times on the shoot that I was impressed by someone asking the 'big' life questions at a very young age. While Rebecca was exploring the meaning of life, I was filling my head with Chekhov monologues and going through a very unfortunate phase of drinking a lot of laxative tea. I'd only just walked away from the Church, but it would be years before I questioned that decision or consciously experienced any kind of a feeling of loss about it. Maybe I was only doing that now.

The biggest challenge for Rebecca (and most nuns, I would imagine) has been turning her back on the idea of family and a partner. She talked freely about being in love since becoming a nun, but I got the feeling that she didn't leave the convent because one man wasn't enough for her. I don't mean her vagina is a Venus flytrap, and that she would just suck men dry and then discard them. I believe she thinks that it's unrealistic to imagine that one person can fulfil all your needs for life. That's something I agree with. These women all strike me as feminists.

I joined the ladies for a liturgy in their prayer room. Rebecca at one point referred to Catholicism being in her DNA and that's something I more than understand. I was uncomfortable praying – I couldn't even bring myself to make the sign of the cross, because I thought that it would be hypocritical – yet it was all so familiar. It wasn't only out of respect for those wonderful women that I didn't just want to go through the motions, either. I have to admit that it was out of some sort of respect for the religion to which I devoted the first eighteen years of my life.

They completely disarmed me when they offered up a prayer for me, and then for the whole team and the success of the series. I asked them to get me a husband, too – well, whatever works. I later found out that they'd continued to pray for us, and that we came in number two after remembering the dead and the suffering. Rebecca finally had to suggest that maybe there were some slightly needier people than me and the film crew on their list. I don't know if that's fair. If those ladies don't keep petitioning the Lord for me, I might wind up having to appear on a reality TV show with Lara Bingle and Merv Hughes.

I've seen Rebecca a couple of times since our initial introduction and I like to think that the friendship will continue. I don't know that she has finished her journey yet, and she clearly has her reservations about the Church. I'm not about to take my vows, but I was honestly struck more by the similarities between Rebecca and me than the differences. Clearly, we both have some sort of yearning for 'a purpose' or meaning in our lives (although it took me longer than her to work that out), and maybe, to some extent, we're both questioning how we have arrived at this point of our lives without partners or a family. I know many single women around my age who are dealing with these issues, and maybe what we are 'missing' is the thing that Rebecca has that takes her out of her own head, by thinking of others and some sort of bigger picture. I doubt she's ever looked in the mirror and thought, 'Maybe God would find me more attractive if I had some Botox.' (Although possibly it's the frozen faces of those statues of Mary that have inspired people like Sandra Bullock.)

Meeting those women and talking about the religion of my youth made me almost miss it. Maybe I don't believe in the god I grew up with, but it strikes me that someone like Rebecca doesn't really, either. For a split second, I wondered if it was possible to just take the bits of Catholicism that I like and work with those. Apparently, the Dalai Lama said that people from the West should look for answers in the traditions that they know, and maybe there's something to that.

As I entered the church to talk to Father Gerry Gleeson, I was again struck by how I can't walk into one of these buildings without experiencing so many emotions. Part of me loves them – it's hard to deny that most places of worship have a sort of tranquillity to them, which must surely be brought about by the people who have prayed there and believed that they were tapping into some sort of grace – and part of me wants to run screaming from the building and have lesbian sex with an unmarried gorilla.

I was more nervous conducting this interview than any other. I knew that Gerry and I would disagree on many areas and yet I didn't want to be disrespectful, because I'm hardwired to treat priests well. On some level, I suppose I have a kind of grudging respect for anyone who has dedicated their entire life to their idea of God. It must take a kind of courage that I certainly don't possess.

Gerry is a reasonable, clever man. He studied at Cambridge and lectures in philosophy and ethics. I liked him, but it didn't take long for my anger about the doctrine of the Church to be stirred up. This made me very uncomfortable. Issues like contraception and abortion are always going to rile me. The thinking seems to be that God vowed to watch over the Church, so whatever is happening is somehow his will. I fail to understand how a hierarchy of men can dictate to women about their bodies. God may not be fallible, but people certainly are – surely it is time to look at the Church's failings? Why am I wasting my breath? Talking to Gerry reminded me of the problems I will always have with it, such as its misogyny and homophobia. He even spoke of the possibility of being reunited with our bodies after death, which made me want to give John Travolta a call to say that maybe the whole Scientology thing wasn't so ludicrous after all (although about seventeen of his film choices have been).

I agreed with some of Gerry's points about society in general. It was hard to argue when he said that maybe we're not coping well with sexuality as a whole and that people are often after quick fixes. What I don't understand, though, is a Church that excludes. I have no idea whether Jesus existed or not, but Catholicism today seems very far removed from the teachings originally made in his name.

Gerry certainly took me back to the negative feelings I'd had about the Church at eighteen, but I've let a lot of my anger go. I'm not a fan of the institution, but there are a lot of great practising Catholics out there, and while I might question their choice, I no longer dismiss it. (Although, with no offence to my spiritual adviser friend, I think I'm still more likely to give Curly head than return to Catholicism.)

EPISODE 2: NOTHING

This was the episode where we looked at my pursuit of boys and booze as an alternative to believing in anything. A nice combination of the two occurred when I attended a singles murder/mystery evening. While I met some terrific people, alcohol is the only way to survive one of these things. I should probably admit that while we filmed this night largely for laughs, I truly did still fantasise about meeting someone. Mr Right might not be the answer, but when you've gone to the trouble of dressing up as a Viking (my allotted character was an opera singer), you're at least hoping for a root.

This was also the episode where we looked at atheism. One of the problems we had while editing the show was that we had way too much material for our six episodes, so we had to drop the footage of our night spent with 'Atheists in the Pub'.

It's exactly that: a bunch of atheists meeting once a month in a pub to talk about being an atheist, and a whole lot of other stuff, I'm sure. When most of them reacted to just the title of my TV show as if I'd said I was about to start worshipping a smurf, I was reminded of how scathing I'd been in my twenties, not only about Catholicism, but of everything from Buddhism to meditation. I didn't blame them. One young woman had grown up in an American fundamentalist Christian family, while another particularly strident non-believer (who said he felt sorry for me) was escaping an oppressive church upbringing in the Philippines. He told me that when he finally rejected his religion, he found it so confronting that he was violently ill. Now that really is a crippling Catholic hangover.

I completely understand the need to reject any kind of belief system, or even an interest in one, after you walk away from years of feeling like you've had a religion shoved down your throat. And it also makes sense to me that you need to work out exactly where your anger is directed: family, culture, the institution, yourself? Is there anything you can salvage from those years? All of that takes time (and, in my case, booze and a long stretch of behaving like a fuckwit).

I know that a lot of my strident atheism was more of a reaction to my past than a carefully considered view. But while I could relate to the atheists, the evening confirmed for me that I may have had no idea what I believed in, but I no longer wanted it to be absolutely nothing.

EPISODE 3: SEEKERS

During my atheist period, I'd often dismissed people's practices and beliefs out of hand; essentially, there was what I believed – nothing – and everything else was clearly horseshit. As I got more involved with yoga, I didn't check my scepticism at the door and suddenly start wearing mauve (in fact, one of the many aspects I like about Eastern philosophy is that it encourages you to question and experience things for yourself and not just blindly believe anything). But it did make me realise that maybe it hadn't just been my hips that needed opening up. Yoga had made me curious, so the third episode reflected my new willingness to try just about anything. There was clearly a lot of rubbish swept under the New Age rug, but maybe it wasn't all crap, and I was sure I would encounter some sincere and good people when we travelled to – where else? – Byron Bay.

I tried everything from 'gong therapy' to a night of healing with some men and women who believe that they channel higher beings (and that they are going to be rescued by spaceships when the world ends on 21 December 2012). I did some shamanic journeying, had my life aligned and tried some tantric massage. Some of the people set off my alarm bells, but some of it made me feel good, like the gong therapy, because it was really just a soothing meditation. The tantric massage, which involved me being virtually nude in front of the camera, made me realise that I'm not destined for a career in porn – a devastating blow.

Many people in Byron have given up their old lives of working nine to five, because they found it unfulfilling or because, again, sickness or the death of someone close to them had made them question their happiness and what they found satisfying. One of the astrologers who now lives at this seaside town had been a very successful car salesman. Presumably, despite his money and business achievements, he felt something was missing. I once read that the only thing that makes you question yourself more than not getting what you want out of life is getting it. (That's not a Third World problem, admittedly: 'Oh no, I've suddenly got food and water, now I don't know what to do!') Anna and Steve, the people behind the gong therapy, have both had health scares and their technique – which involves relaxing while experiencing the vibrations from an incredible assortment of musical instruments being played around you – literally resonates with them. Anna enjoyed an incredible euphoria when she first tried it, as it almost made time stop for her. They refer to it as 'vibrational cleansing'. All I know is that when they put a bowl over my head and hit it, I felt as though Lurch from *The Addams Family* had moved into my skull. But after I got to lie down and listen to the strange music produced by their kooky gongs, I felt very relaxed and full of energy. This was the one thing I tried in Byron that everyone in the crew liked the look of.

I did some shamanic journeying with Darpan. This is an ancient ritual that involved everything from deep-throat singing to guitar playing, burning candles and herbs, and lingering a lot around my chakras. I found this really relaxing too, probably because I was lying down again. It could certainly be argued that if the incantations had been replaced by a banana lounge and a mai tai it would probably have had the same effect, but I liked Darpan. He'd grown up Catholic, but his searching had led him to this and because it works for him he wants to share it with other people.

I think that's what a lot of them are doing: trying to make

a living out of techniques that they believe genuinely work. Obviously there are people who just want to make money, too. One woman used a pendant that she waved above a board with words and symbols on it and told me she had seen this process cure cancer in ten minutes. If the pendant was so powerful, I wondered, why hadn't it let her know that she really needed to take a shower?

Yet, I met a couple that thought this same person was 'incredible' and had changed their lives. If you really want to be healed, then you'll be healed; if you want aliens to speak through you, then I guess they will. A woman at a place called the Lotus Temple told me that she'd found herself walking around her home in Melbourne shouting, 'Why are we here? What's the point?' before she was 'led' to Byron.

I encountered a lot of people seeking, looking for an explanation, and many seemed to think that they'd found it. I wouldn't be surprised if five years from now they believed in something quite different (especially after the fizzer of 21 December 2012). My attitude to a lot of this New Age whacky stuff is pretty similar to what it was when I used to write routines about it, although it's significant that I would no longer make the people the butt of my jokes. I might think that a lot of what I encountered makes as much sense as the Fat Zapper, but at least these people are trying. Who am I to judge? Something psychic John Edward said, when we interviewed him for the show, was that there is a big difference between being a cynic and being a sceptic, and I like to think that I am now the latter. (The trouble is, after striking the New Age off my list, and the selfish deaths of my parents, I'm fast running out of material.)

Speaking of which, I thought a lot of Mum throughout the series. As I say, she was quite the seeker herself and I don't think she would have been entirely out of place in somewhere like Byron, so this was also the episode where I followed in her footsteps, with both re-birthing and the Charismatic Movement.

I attempted re-birthing with a lovely woman called Pauline. It essentially involves her guiding you through a form of breathing that supposedly helps clear the trauma of birth and early childhood.

I had always found Mum's attempt at this hilarious. You're meant to recall your own birth, but, never one to follow the norm, Mum had remembered giving birth to me and had set her memories down in a graphic and disturbing letter when I was in my early twenties. This was to become even more confusing when I found out I was adopted.

We wound up with me in a bath breathing through a snorkel, which was actually just giving me more trauma, as I felt like I was drowning, but once we moved to the bed for more lying down, I found it pretty enjoyable. Mainly because the weird hyperventilated breathing, combined with the recent heat of the bath, made me feel pleasantly light-headed, and a little stoned. Pauline said this was me releasing past toxins. I just wished I hadn't spent all that money on dope over the years, when all I needed was a bathtub.

As much as I liked Pauline, this was all pretty difficult to take seriously. She had placed a picture of a particularly foxy guru near the bath. She said that he was the founder of re-birthing, still alive after thousands of years – let's hope he had a superannuation plan. She then explained that the whole point of this technique was immortality, and that she had no interest in the afterlife because she was never going to experience it. Ballsy stuff to say in front of a camera. I did wonder if Mum had known this, or if she'd been content with getting a little off her head and spinning her daughter a load of old codswallop.

She tried something else not long before she died, and that was throwing her lot in with the Catholic Charismatic Renewal Movement. These are Catholics who, not content with just the mass, like to get together and make sounds a bit like a theremin. They speak in tongues.

Despite the suspicions they must have had (if you spoke in tongues, would you let a comedian with a camera crew crash your service?), people were extremely warm and friendly – I couldn't have been more ill at ease. Throughout the shoot, my intention was never to set anyone up or send up their choices, yet this was one occasion where I feared that they would be able to look into my eyes and tell that I thought they were insane. Much of my prejudice came from my feelings about Pentecostal churches like Hillsong. They seem to combine the worst ideas of Catholicism with creationism and a slick, moneymaking ethos that makes me a little sick.

There was a more varied group of people than I was expecting in the little room off a seventies church (no slickness here). Mostly, the congregation was older but there were different nationalities and age groups and the evening really revealed more about my intolerance. This is a dreadful thing to say, but what made my alarm bells ring more than anything was how HAPPY people seemed to be. I wondered what was wrong with them. I was especially suspicious when they greeted a couple who had returned from a holiday with real enthusiasm and interest. No-one really wants to hear about someone else's vacation – these people were obviously deeply disturbed. And when I saw some young attractive women, I thought, 'Shouldn't you be out binge drinking and having sex that you'll regret for the rest of your lives? If the Holy Spirit is the only thing entering you, it's time to take a good, hard look at yourselves.'

When the evening got under way, at first it was people speaking and reading scripture. It was all very familiar, until at some point it was as if someone had said, 'Start wailing and singing like a possessed Gibb brother . . . now!' And it began. Even the people who weren't 'speaking' were putting their arms in the air and swaying and having some sort of dramatic experience, whatever it was. And then the healing started. Before I knew it, a woman was asking me if she could lay her hands on me – what could I say? I was in way too deep, so I let her lay her palms on my head. To the best of my knowledge, all this did was make my hair look a little flat, but it was still a kind gesture.

While the speaking in tongues was a little confronting, I was impressed by the fact that, certainly on the night we were in attendance, the thrust of the service was about love and forgiveness. Not a bad message. Allan Panozza did most of the talking, and has been involved in the movement since the seventies. He's like the grandfather you wish you'd had, someone you know immediately is a fundamentally good person. He seemed as surprised as anyone that his faith had led him down this path. When he first started speaking in tongues, he said, 'I don't know who was more surprised – me or the Holy Spirit.' Because that's what they believe is happening: the Spirit enters them and they have no control over it.

Many of the people I spoke to had interesting stories, but almost all of them had come to the CCR after a low point in their lives, or when they were on the verge of leaving the Church altogether. One man had attended on the suggestion of his sister and thought that the people he met needed help, but he said that he found himself down the front the following week 'weeping like a baby'. There is not a doubt in my mind that these people were looking for something and they had found it. Friends, a community and (they believe) a tangible manifestation of the love of God – that's a pretty big night out for anyone.

I told Allan about my mother and asked him what he thought happened when we die. He assured me that no matter how much Mum loved God, He loved her more, and that she would be sitting up there in heaven with him now. Unfortunately, I think that's a load, but it was nice to hear just the same. Alan really won me over when the cameras stopped rolling. He gave me his card and said I could call him any time if I wanted to talk about anything. I absolutely knew that he meant this and while I doubt I'll ever call, I've kept the card.

What moved me most about the whole evening was thinking about Mum. I felt I understood why she had attended these meetings. She would have loved the theatre of it but, as happy as she might now be sitting next to Jesus, I think she really went along because she wanted to be healed – she wanted to live and be well again. Doctors had failed her, so she reached out to something else. And maybe that something else, Catholicism, had always been a genuine comfort to her without me realising it, even if I don't believe it gave her everything she craved, which is why she gave quite a few things a try.

When I was a kid I thought most of her dabblings were bonkers and yet her death actually prompted me to start searching in a similar way. And this, in turn, had made me realise that I could no longer discount a person's way of making sense of life as quickly as I had in the past, whether that involved gongs, snorkels or the Holy Spirit.

EPISODE 4: STILLNESS

Episode four was about the madness of career. Delightful comedian Frank Woodley compared what we do to being a monkey with a mango. He said that when you cracked a joke on stage and people made this weird sound called laughter, it's like you're a monkey and you're driving the other monkeys nuts by pulling a piece of fruit out from behind your back, and then hiding it behind you again. It was good to know that after about seventeen years I had finally worked out that there might be more to life than acting like a chimpanzee.

The rest of the episode was dedicated to one of the most affecting experiences of the series: spending a couple of days with three female Aboriginal elders just outside Alice Springs. Up until recently, I knew nothing about Aboriginal people. Now I know next to nothing, but it's still an improvement. Like most left-leaning, arty white wankers, I'm riddled with guilt about our Indigenous population, but I didn't have one Aboriginal friend. I did know, however, that I couldn't do a show about spirituality and not at least attempt to spend some time with the people who've been here so much longer than us.

About six months before we started filming, I volunteered to help run a couple of workshops about stand-up comedy for Deadly Funny, the indigenous stand-up competition that's part of the Melbourne International Comedy Festival. I'd never run a workshop before, incidentally, and didn't have the slightest idea of what I was doing.

The first night, I remember being the only white person in a room with twelve Aboriginal people, nursing a hangover and thinking, 'Holy fuck, how have I reached my age and never been in a room with maybe even three Indigenous people? I'm a nice person. I want to do the right thing, I mean, I feel bad – isn't that enough? Are you going to tell me that maybe I should've made some sort of effort before now?'

I have no idea if I taught those poor budding comedians anything, but I certainly learnt a couple of things. One of the older women said to me, 'We understand your humour but you don't understand ours.' What could I say to that? No, of course we don't. Most of us don't understand anything about you. At the quarter final, I sat in the audience and listened to some of the men tell stories about police busts and prison time while a fourteen-year-old boy talked about being a father.

I was also a moron, of course. I remember one of the women telling me about how she'd set up a website and I was effusive with my praise. This was because I can barely work a computer, so the idea of someone creating an actual site on one always impresses me. As soon as I said it, though, I thought, 'Oh my God, she thinks I'm being patronising, but if I explain myself and say that I wasn't being patronising, won't that actually *be* patronising? . . . FOR THE LOVE OF GOD, I'M NOT A RACIST!'

While running the workshops, I got a glimpse of the incredible sense of family and connection there is in their culture, so this was a sliver of the newfound knowledge that I took to Alice Springs when filming the TV show. Our director, Brendan, has worked a lot with Indigenous people, so he and I, along with our field producer, Jo, went up to Alice a day early, in the hope of meeting the elder women who were going to try to teach me something about Aboriginal spirituality. We'd been told by our tour organiser, Jungala, that there was every chance I wouldn't meet anyone that night, and a slight chance that I wouldn't meet anyone at all.

Jungala and his partner, Colleen, run the only Indigenous tourist business in the area, setting up 'experiences' for non-Indigenous people. He was the one who told us that if I wanted to learn anything about this culture's spirituality, I would have to learn from women.

I was terrified. When we met Jungala and Colleen, I barely spoke as Jungala drove us out to his cousin Steven's farm. He's the traditional owner of this land and it's his wife, Gloria, and two of her buddies who would be taking me under their wing. At least when I was attempting to impart some wisdom about comedy to Aboriginal people, I was dealing with a topic I actually know something about. In the desert, I was stripped of everything but my insecurities.

We set out the next day and it took me a while to realise just how extraordinary the land is. There'd been a lot of rain, so the desert was actually very green and full of wildflowers. But it's the contrast of the blue sky with the red earth that's dazzling and there's a kind of stillness here that makes you feel very small. I think it's because you realise how utterly helpless you are in the middle of this enormous landmass – there's very little about it you can control and you're completely dependent on it.

I'd never camped in my life. I spent the first twenty-four hours in the desert holding rocks to my ear and saying, 'Room service?' In fact, the few holidays I'd gone on in the past had involved simply shifting what I did in my living room (drinking, smoking and watching television) to a hotel room. That was money well spent.

Like something out of a movie, later on the second afternoon the three ladies who were going to teach me appeared: Gloria, Maggie and Beryl. Maggie is Beryl's mother and neither of them speaks much English, so Gloria did most of the talking. They appeared from out of the red dust in dresses and beanies, while I just continued to feel scared, guilty and trivial. The women were gentle and generous. I never stopped feeling like an intruder.

The next day, the women welcomed us to country with a smoking ceremony. I can now return to that land anytime. It's hard to understand the connection they have. Everything around them seems to have a story behind it. It's okay to walk up that hill, but not another one. It's best to travel in groups because a spirit might take you. Some stories are too dangerous to repeat . . . the Dreaming is ongoing and everywhere. It's a long way from home for me, and a long way from my understanding.

They took me to dig up honey ants and, sitting knee-deep in red dirt, eating these delicious insects out of the ground, I marvelled that life had led me to this point. 'Waiter, there's an ant in my mouth!'

After only about thirty-six hours, I don't know whether it was the company or the desert, or both, but I remember thinking that I'd rarely felt so completely relaxed and happy. If I thought to think at all, it was only to become aware of the fact that I wasn't thinking.

It was an experience I will not forget. Theirs is a culture that thrives on mutual respect and responsibility, for the land and for each other. It seems a much healthier way to live, with so much less emphasis on 'I'. The traditions are beautiful. I feel no less guilty, but it has given me a hunger to want to spend more time in the Centre. I want to understand more about this land and these people.

We also interviewed Mark Yettica Paulson, who told me, just after our plane had landed in Alice Springs, that I didn't need to come to the desert to experience his people's spirituality. Couldn't he have told me that before I bought the ticket? He meant, of course, that it's everywhere: in the cities, and the rivers that run through them, and sometimes we need to take our shoes off and remember the land that we're walking on.

This episode ended with a newfound appreciation of my own country, but it also made me realise that it's possible to learn about and appreciate traditions that aren't necessarily your own – although, in this case, maybe they should be.

EPISODE 5: MIND

If I have a favourite episode, it's probably the one about yoga and meditation. I went into the series already loving the former and wanting to know a lot more about the latter.

Yoga is meant to lead to meditation and I think one of the reasons I'd fallen for it pretty quickly was because I'd read that it was about stilling the mind. For a long time, I had no idea what this meant, but gee, did I like the sound of it.

I'm very grateful to my mind. It's helped me put on pants and write the odd joke, but it can also be a bit like Mickey Rourke's face – an inexplicable, disturbing mess.

My mind was at its worst when it came to performing. I would wake up gripped with a kind of terror: rapidly beating heart, no appetite, ceaseless thoughts about the show, and all coupled with the thought that these reactions were ridiculous. I was telling jokes to some people who'd paid money to see me, not being fired out of a cannon into the mouth of a hungry shark. But trying to think my way out of the nerves never worked. The last time I toured, I saw a doctor about it, vainly thinking that beta-blockers might be a solution. The panic attacks after my father's death had made an existing problem worse, and when I told the doctor that the whole issue had been going on for about ten years, he asked if I'd ever seen any other health professionals to try and get some help. Astonishingly, the answer was no – am I a cretin? I think because it wasn't a physical issue, I thought that I should just soldier on and pull myself together. On some level, I probably even saw it as merely being weak.

But who doesn't worry? While we certainly have a high standard of living in the West, life can still be pretty scary. I think most of us deal with some sort of stress almost all the time. There are obvious worries, like making a living and keeping a roof over your head, and possibly your family's, but reading the newspaper is generally enough to make me want to put my hands on my head, walk outside of my home and declare that I just give up. There is always some new nightmare that awaits us, whether it's financial disaster, a tsunami or a new crop of terrorists. And frankly, some days, I can just shit myself walking into Coles. Sometimes the thought of having to make even the most basic conversation with a stranger is more than I can take.

So episode five was where I tried some serious meditation and spoke to someone who has made it a big part of his life: ex-captain of the Sydney Swans, Brett Kirk. Of all the people we spoke to, Brett got the greatest audience response (I think even straight men want to sleep with Brett now). We wanted to talk to someone who had a spiritual practice but who didn't, as was the case with one of our interviewees, drive a van with 'OM' number plates. I don't think you can get more mainstream, in this country, than a footballer. These guys, sorry to say, are generally better known for getting drunk and photographing their penis than they are for having an interest in Eastern philosophy.

But not Brett Kirk. The death of a football mentor many

years ago made him question the way he was living his life and has led him to a spiritual practice that involves yoga, meditation, an interest in Buddhism and a continuing search. I don't doubt that Brett has his moments, but he seems very much together. When he talks to you, he really listens, and I'm not in any way surprised that he was renowned for his complete focus on the football field. He's passionate about his practice and I admire the way he approaches it with the discipline of an athlete. Every morning he's up at 5.30 doing his yoga and meditation, which includes a daily affirmation. He shared that with us and I honestly thought that I was going to burst into tears. It was full of gratitude and a desire to live a good life in the moment, which is all we really have. Maybe it was powerful because he has said it so often, but for whatever reason, it just felt like he was talking from his core and I was listening with mine. (It's not lost on me that Brett is also an extremely hot ex-footy player, and I'm sure he knows that if his wonderful wife ever slips into a coma, I'll be there for him.)

As I say, I'm not the only one that felt this. Brett inspired a lot of people who watched the show because he was sincere and seemed to actually embody the compassion and presence of which he spoke. He's a wonderful example of what some sort of spirituality can do for a person and if he wanted to start his own religion I think a lot of people would sign up on the spot. The other interesting aspect about him is that he's still questioning, and I really do admire anyone that's not quick to settle on one answer.

Brett was proof of what regular meditation can do, so I jumped in the deep end and signed up for a ten-day silent Vipassana retreat. They sounded like meditation boot camps, a kind of Buddhist *Survivor*, and I thought that was exactly what I needed. I'd certainly meditated before, but never with any consistency. I was less routine with it than I was with waxing, which is something I can often leave until I look like a yeti. But meditation had interested me for some time and I knew that to reap any rewards from it, you had to do it regularly.

All I knew about the retreat was that it was ten days of meditating and that you weren't allowed to do anything else: no speaking, reading, music, yoga, nothing. Most people I mentioned it to thought that I was insane for attempting it and, more than anything, baulked at the idea of silence. I suspected that that side of it wouldn't bother me, but I can't say that I anticipated it like I would have a trip to the Maldives. And certainly, relaxing is not the word I would use to describe the experience I wound up having.

The retreat was about an hour out of Melbourne and I knew that it would be cold, so I set off to buy thermal underwear and more tracksuits. That was the best money I've ever spent. For the entire ten days it was wet and FREEZING. At one point I was wearing three pairs of socks, long johns, pants, a spencer, two tops, a cardigan, a track-suit top, winter coat, scarf and gloves. I forgot what I looked like from the neck down, and by about the fourth day that was probably a blessing. Fate really was shining on me because Country Road was having a sale, so I wound up with two black velour tracksuits for a song. All I needed was a four-wheel drive, blonde hair and a face as expressive as a fridge, and I could've been a wealthy mother of three. The only down side was that the woman who sold them to me told me that her mother had attempted a Vipassana retreat and had missed talking and drinking so much that she'd gotten her family to bust her out on day three.

I arrived at about two on the first day with the crew, we did a couple of interviews and then they left me to it. Most people were put in dorms, but the older you are, the more privileges you seem to get, so I was lucky enough to have my own room, which looked like my idea of a prison cell: a single bed, a small table and a window. While I was impossibly jealous of the women who had ensuites (the rest of us used the toilet and shower block), I was incredibly grateful that I didn't have to share the results of the high-fibre diet with anyone else in the middle of the night – 'silence' really flew out the window (and my arse) at that point.

The 'Noble Silence' didn't start until eight that evening, so women being women, we all sat around and talked about ourselves and why we were there. Yet again, it was a mixed bag, to say the least. I was surprised by the number of tourists. These places are all over the world, so I don't know why you would come to Australia and spend, in one woman's case, your last ten days abroad in silence and drinking a shitload of fennel tea.

While a couple of people simply wanted to do the retreat because they had an interest in Buddhism and were curious about what they'd heard about Vipassana, I think it's fair to say that a lot of the women were hoping for something quite profound to happen. One older woman had recently lost a brother and a daughter, another had given up her only child for adoption and had failed to re-connect with her, and yet another said that she was simply consumed with negativity despite having a good life.

The place is completely gender-segregated: the only time you saw the men was in the meditation hall, and even then we were on different sides. On the final day, I realised that most of them were tourists too, and some of them were so attractive that they could've handed out ten-by-four glossies of themselves. I was old enough to be their incredibly hot mother – what is it with these kids? Who went meditating in their twenties? Don't you just turn to it when you've finally worked out that booze and pills don't work? I found the whole segregation aspect hilarious, not having experienced it since I went to an all-girl school. At times in the hall, I was so bored and frustrated that I fantasised about walking over to the guys' side and saying, 'Okay, who wants to sleep with me? You – old, hippie guy with the spearmint culottes and ponytail – outside, let's go.'

My overwhelming thought on the first night was that I had no clue what I was in for. This is a feeling I've experienced many, many times in my life. I have a tendency to mentally underprepare, whether I'm starting a new job, a new relation-ship or travelling to a country where no-one speaks English. It's never until the instant of arriving or committing that I think, 'Wow, I haven't thought this through at all and I reckon I could be totally screwed.'

We meditated for a couple of hours but the next day was officially day one. This was the schedule:

4.30–6.30 meditation
6.30–8.00 breakfast
8.00–9.00 group meditation
9.00–11.00 meditation
11.00–1.00 lunch
1.00–2.30 meditation
2.30–3.30 group meditation
3.30–5.00 meditation
5.00–6.00 'dinner'
6.00–7.00 group meditation
7.15–8.20 Goenka discourse
8.30–9.00 group meditation
9.30 lights out

For ten days.

As you can see, it was a pretty varied timetable. Ten and a half hours of meditation a day. If it wasn't group meditation, you could do it in your room, but I only did this from 4.30 to

6.30, when to the untrained eye it might have looked like I'd simply said, 'Fuck it, I'm staying in bed for two more hours.' I only did that a couple of times, in truth, when I was either exhausted (believe me, it is exhausting) or just pissed off. I reasoned that I had another eight and a half hours to make up for it.

These retreats were started by a man called Goenka, from Myanmar. He was a wealthy businessman who suffered from chronic headaches that were eventually cured by this form of meditation, and so he made it his mission to embrace Buddhism and spread the word about how the technique could change your life. There is no fee, but you can make a donation at the end if you desire. I'm imagining that most schools have the same timetable and approach throughout the world (although I read about one in Italy where people were, of course, allowed to smoke). There is a 'teacher' at the front of the meditation hall who you can speak to at lunchtime, but the entire course is directed by Goenka himself, via audio and video tapes. I never went to the teacher with an issue, but apparently her response to every query was the same: 'Just watch the breath.'

So the first morning we were all sitting in the hall, following the instructions of a man who sounded like a cross between Barry White and an Indian Bob Hawke. In other words, really fucking annoying. This wasn't helped by his tendency to say everything three times: 'If you do not change your way of thinking, you will be miserable . . . miserable . . . miserable.' 'Make sure you work diligently . . . diligently . . . diligently.' I often found myself thinking, 'Why don't you get rooted . . . rooted . . . rooted.' On top of this, his directions were often broken up with nose clearing and burping. Apparently, being enlightened must preclude the use of tissues, Quick-Eze and MANNERS.

Breakfast and lunch were healthy vegetarian meals, but 'dinner' was two pieces of fruit. The first day, after chowing down on my second apple, I thought, 'I've made a huge mistake. And I think I could be involved in a cult.' I shouldn't have complained – if you've done the course more than once, you don't even get fruit, just warm lemon water. At times, I wasn't sure if I was on a spiritual retreat or being held as a prisoner of war.

I had no intention of leaving and thankfully my feelings of desolation were lifted on the first night, when we watched the video of Goenka speaking for an hour. He was still belching and sniffing away, but he was warm and funny, and radiated love and compassion. He explained that the technique was taught by Buddha and that it's about leading a moral, good life, serving others and disciplining the mind. I couldn't argue with any of that. The five tenets we agreed to follow for the next nine days were: no killing, no stealing, no lying, no sexual misconduct and no intoxicants. You can imagine which one of those I broke within an hour of leaving. (That's right, I killed a guy.)

We spent the first THREE DAYS concentrating simply on the area just below our nostrils – no wonder they don't tell you that going in. Then we finally learnt Vipassana, which is essentially scanning the entire body for sensations. Once you start to feel tiny electrical currents throughout your skin, you start to 'sweep' the body and then scan beyond the surface and into your entire form. For example, you start off just being aware of the skin on your leg, but eventually you are aware of the entire leg. In the end, hopefully, there are no blockages (areas of pain or numbness), and it feels like the entire body has dissolved into a series of waves or atoms. Sometimes the sensations were extremely pleasant, sometimes parts of my body fell asleep and, for the most part, I was in excruciating pain. Here's a tip, too: I spent the first three or four days trying to work out the right way to sit and the right way to combine cushions so as to feel comfortable while meditating – THERE IS NO RIGHT WAY.

This is the other chestnut no-one tells you. It's really hard sitting in the same position for hours. Obviously, you can move, but nothing really helps and after the first few days there were three sittings of 'strong determination' every day. These last for an hour and you're encouraged to be completely still. I'm sure everyone had different areas of discomfort – for me it was my lower back. The pain was so bad that I thought I was on my way to a wheelchair.

The idea is to realise how all sensations are impermanent. The main purpose seems to be to break the patterns of attachment and aversion that we have in our minds. Of course, if you felt something nice you wanted it to last, and if you were in agony you would sit there making your pain so much worse, by think-

ing, 'WHEN IS THIS GOING TO END? THIS IS TORTURE.
I CAN'T THINK OF ANYTHING OTHER THAN THE PAIN,
THE PAIN AND THE PAIN.'

The bigger picture was that we were meant to lose all sense
of 'I', comprehend the impermanence of everything, including
ourselves, and cultivate love and compassion. I didn't necessarily agree with the 'science' of it all. (We're meant to be made
up of particles called 'calapas', and the pains we experienced
were meant to be manifestations of old habits of craving and
aversion. Calapa trapa.) But I liked the fundamental ideas
very much. For me, it was more about exploring the nature of
thought; learning how we can make a situation, whether it's a
sore leg or an irritating person or a performance, so much worse
by negatively fixating on it.

There were good days and bad. Day four was a nightmare.
It was like all my negative thoughts got together and had a huge
party. I knew I had some self-loathing issues, but this was like
watching my mental dialogue under a microscope, while stoned
on some hydroponic grass. It was so relentless that I remember thinking it was futile to even imagine I could change my
life. Why not just go back to wiping myself out, if this was the
alternative? It was just my usual string of personal abuse (you're
stupid, you're ugly and – one of my father's favourite lines –
why can't you be more like Tina Arena?), but I had nothing to
distract me from these thoughts and it made me feel completely
helpless. If my negative mind and I had been engaged in some

sort of battle, it had definitely won. I really couldn't see how things would ever improve, and yet the next day was completely different. The thoughts were still there but they didn't bother me anymore. I could sit back and watch them come and go and not get involved, and I actually started to experience tiny breaks in the relentless flow.

Day seven was another killer – more mind manipulation. My back pain was so bad that I was convinced I was going to have to leave and see a doctor, or else risk some permanent damage. It was no worse than anyone else's, but I believed I was the only person who urgently needed medical attention. (Mind you, I saw one of the younger women crying, talking to herself and walking backwards at one point, but I figured she needed attention of a different kind.)

There were some pretty nice moments, as well. Sometimes you would hear a bird sing or even a person cough and be overwhelmed with the feeling of being a part of something outside your self. Sometimes during a break you would look at a blossom or a flower as though you'd never seen one before, and surrender to the almost incredible fact that it exists. You'd stop feeling annoyed by the rain and marvel at it instead. (Why hadn't someone told me this was possible without MDMA?)

Halfway through day ten, the 'Noble Silence' ended . . . and did the ladies talk! It was wonderful just to hear laughter again and to realise that all the pain and emotional drama you'd gone through had been experienced by everyone else as well.

We all thought that the person sitting next to us had remained perfectly still for hours at a time while we were the only ones wriggling like a ten-year-old. Everyone thought it was hard, but was glad that they'd done it. The weirdest moment for me was when a German tourist asked me what I did for a living. She couldn't believe I was a comedian. She told me she'd spent two days observing me, trying to work out my profession, and she'd decided I was either a policewoman, an undertaker or that I worked in an egg factory. If that's the vibe I'm giving off, it could explain a lot.

I didn't miss talking, or TV, or alcohol (except when we first learnt the Vipassana technique and had to sit completely motionless for two hours – I was so delighted I'd gotten through it, I felt I'd earned a stiff drink, but instead I got a banana). I did miss reading, music, writing and yoga.

By day ten, I was amazed at how easy the 'strong determination' sittings had become. I don't think that I was in any less pain but I'd found a way of dealing with it. It was like the negative thoughts: if I didn't hold onto the pain, it ceased to be a problem. I had a real sense of clarity and thought that maybe this technique was for me. Certainly, meditation was something I wanted to continue with.

The next day I felt a little sad that after sharing this experience, a lot of the women just drifted away without even saying goodbye. Or maybe I was just pissed off that I was left to clean the toilets on my own.

I wasn't looking forward to the crew arriving and having to talk about what had just occurred. I'd enjoyed the quiet. Of course, as soon as the camera started rolling you couldn't shut me up, and apparently, on the drive back, I continued to talk like a speed freak.

Buddhism believes in both wisdom and compassion; i.e., sort your own nonsense out so you can be vaguely useful to others. The retreat confirmed for me how important it is to understand the way your mind works, and its limits. Most of us have experienced the negative impact our thoughts can have on us, whether it's obsessing on a pain or fear, or some story about ourselves, whether true or not. I've certainly managed to turn a person not returning my phone call for a day or two into a confirmation that I'm a worthless human being not worthy of love, only to discover, in one case, that their kid had put their phone in the washing machine. More and more, I wanted to take my mind a little less seriously, and this episode helped me realise that was possible.

EPISODE 6: REVELATION

The path may be the goal but, in terms of the TV show, the end of my 'journey' was in India and it was pretty life-changing. As clichéd as it is for a white person to grab a sari and head to that great country to find enlightenment, it had seemed appropriate, mainly because of my love of vindaloo, not to mention the great sitcom *It Ain't Half Hot Mum*. And, of course, India is the birthplace of yoga. I was increasingly interested in Buddhism, as well, and so I'd been attracted to the idea of visiting the home of the Mahabohdi Temple – the place where the Buddha became enlightened.

We arrived at seven-thirty at night, and Jo, our field producer, and I immediately headed out of the airport for a cigarette (one of the least spiritual aspects of the shoot was that I took up smoking again). The combination of the heat, fatigue, a few wines on the plane and chronic pollution meant that for my first fifteen minutes in India I thought that instead of gaining consciousness, I was going to lose it completely. It really felt like once I'd left the neutral territory of the airport, India just hit me.

Our hotel was a little metaphor for the country: mystifying yet incredibly polite service, wonderful food in the great restaurant but plaster lying in the middle of opulent corridors, great beds next to phones that didn't work and a shower that was essentially a tap.

It was a full first day. India is the attack on the senses that everyone promises: the bright colours, the smells (urine one minute, spices the next), and the onslaught of people begging or wanting to sell you something. Our director, Brendan, wanted to film me crossing the street and if I ever want to kill myself, this would at least be a colourful way to do it. Crossing the road has never been my forte, so one of the locals looking after us,

Deepak, had to accompany me to ensure I wasn't mown down. It's a country where it pays to be a little bossy. I was bad at putting up a hand to make a car stop, and I was in pain telling people that I didn't want to buy what they had to offer. A nine-year-old girl berated me into buying some necklaces off her and I'm amazed I didn't give her my outfit, my watch and my teeth.

Later that night, we went to a Sufi shrine and it was the first inkling I had that religion is everywhere in this country. The wardrobe department had fitted me out with loose, Indian-type tops and baggy cotton pants. I combined this with a head scarf before entering the shrine and looked like a cross between the Virgin Mary and Tania Zaetta (when she's in Bollywood mode). Men were playing instruments and singing; women cannot enter the actual shrine, so I sat and listened to the music and tried not to look out of place. This was about as likely as the eighties West Indian cricket team fitting in as part of the staff at my old primary school.

One of the first interviews we did on arriving in Delhi was with a Buddhist nun, Sister Robina Courtin. There is much about this philosophy that I like and I was convinced that if I was going to wind up calling myself anything by the end of the series it would be a Buddhist.

Robina is another person who's been searching her whole life. She was born in Melbourne and, like me, wanted to be a Catholic nun at the age of twelve. Unlike me, once she walked away from the Church, she threw herself into everything from sex and drugs to politics, radical lesbian separatism and martial arts. She said she was always looking for truth and a way to explain the world, and when Buddhism found her over thirty years ago, she obviously felt that it was the answer. In her own words, she looks like Ronnie Corbett and she's fast, funny and passionate.

While I'm interested in this ancient philosophy, I do have difficulty with concepts such as reincarnation. By the end of the interview, however, thanks to this articulate woman who I could very much relate to, I was convinced that Buddhism was still worth exploring – even, as she put it, if I'm just a one per cent Buddhist. Not surprisingly, one of the reasons it has always appealed to her is because of the importance placed on meditation in this tradition. 'It enables us to know what the hell is going on inside this crazy mind of ours.'

I'm in touch with this wonderful Buddhist nun and to hear her speak is always inspiring. She's a great advertisement for Buddhism as she radiates a kind of contentment and yet also a passion for living. And while she has embraced this religion as her answer, I believe one of the reasons is because it's a tradition that encourages questioning and a sense of responsibility, something that appeals to me as well. Because it doesn't support the idea of a 'creator', there is no emphasis on a greater power that lies outside of us – that's my understanding of it, anyway. But as with any religion, philosophy and practice are not always in tune.

The next day we headed to Bodh Gaya, the home of the Mahabodhi Temple. Bodh Gaya was certainly a change of pace from Delhi. It's rural and very poor. This was the place where the beggars really affected me. Don't get me wrong, I ignored them, because that's what everyone said to do, and also because I was too shell-shocked to react. By the end of the trip, I was giving money to anyone who asked, but initially I just repressed my horror and guilt.

As usual, repressing didn't work, and I should know – I'm a repressor from way back. An image of a child begging in this place still pops into my head constantly, months later. He was young and his limbs were so deformed that all he could do was crawl along the ground like a crab. I know there are meant to be many fake beggars in India, but this kid wasn't one of them and I walked past him. Incidentally, I don't care if a person is a fake, really. It's not like they chose that over being a lawyer, is it? It's not like they thought, 'Forget Medicine, I'd rather pretend not to be able to walk, and just hang around in dirt and piss all day. Chicks'll love it and I'll get my own bowl!'

The temple was stunning. It's the home of the Bodhi tree (or at least a tree related to it), under which the Buddha became enlightened, along with many other significant sites that were part of his time of awakening. The temple and its grounds teemed with Buddhist monks from all over the world, many of whom had their own temples in and around the town. Despite the number of people, there was a peace there that was hard to miss. It was a beautiful place, although it was sometimes hard to truly appreciate the tranquillity when I was being followed by a camera crew. At least by this stage I'd abandoned caring what I looked like, in terms of worrying about my hair and makeup. (Come to think of it, maybe that happened about twelve years ago.)

We were so busy filming 'finding me' that it was often impossible to really participate in a way that would contribute to that end, but it's a small gripe, and there were still moments where I experienced a glimpse of something, even if it was like seeing someone out of the corner of your eye before they disappear around a bend. At one point, I saw Brendan take a photo on his stills camera, look at it and smile. It broke my heart just for a minute, because there was something so simple and universal in that grin. It was like hearing someone cough during the Vipassana retreat – I was struck by how many times I'd done that, or heard or seen others do it (a cough, a smile, a shrug), and I was struck by how long humans had been doing these tiny gestures for. For a split second, it made me feel a part of something ongoing, of the flow of life that will continue long after I'm gone. And that wasn't terrifying, it was comforting.

We had another member of the team while we were there: Sanjaya, a local who had spent much time at the Temple. He was taken in by a Buddhist monk as a boy (I know, I thought it sounded creepy too, but remember: he's not a Catholic priest), who raised him and taught him about the religion. He is devout and feels indebted to the monk, who changed his life. He is so gentle and when he gave me a perfect leaf that had fallen off the Bodhi tree, I was truly touched. Don't tell Customs, but I still have it. It's in a wooden box next to a statue of Buddha and some Hindu gods, in the room where I practise yoga. It's pretentious, but what else am I going to stick in a yoga room – a sheep's skull and my Iron Maiden CDs?

During the day, we visited a Buddhist-run home for children living with or affected by HIV. We spoke to an Australian woman, Gerri, who volunteers there. She's in her mid thirties, and what I found so impressive about her was that she wasn't inspired to completely change her life by trauma or death. She was happily married to a great guy and loved her job as a horticulturalist, but thought that there must be more to life. Like me, she did the ten-day Vipassana course and it was there that she had the revelation that she should study Buddhism and move to India. I was jealous of her, really (apart from when she told me that when she and her boyfriend were still searching, they would get drunk, argue about whether or not they actually existed, and try and set themselves on fire). She seemed very happy and clear. I think there's something appealing about a revelation that pays off – a light-bulb moment. Gerri never looked back. From the moment she arrived, she felt that India was home. She'll probably have a breakdown, or I'll read about her being charged with drug-smuggling and running a child prostitution ring, but back then, she embodied that movie-like idea of a person who had taken a risk that paid off. It's different for everyone, of course. I met some other Westerners in India who'd done almost exactly what Gerri had, and yet they struck me very differently: one seemed very much to be running away from something, and the other one was just a whacko.

I don't know how many people have those kinds of light-bulb experiences. For most of us, life is just a series of moments that occasionally add up to something, like when I got to meditate under the Bohdi tree the following morning, largely unfilmed. Despite the noise of the many other meditators chanting, sniffing or just generally being alive, it still gave me a sense of peace. It was doubtless the soothing tones of the industrial vacuum cleaner whizzing by that made me feel at one with the universe, or at least with Hoover. It was actually just nice to be surrounded by people all doing the same thing.

Later that day, we interviewed a half-British, half-Indian monk called Kabir. He's a very likable eccentric who, if he loses his way spiritually, would make a great Dr Who. I wanted to embrace Buddhism but I was disconcerted by the worship of Buddha that I saw at the Temple. My Catholic upbringing has put me off the notion of kneeling before any god, and the little I knew of this faith hadn't prepared me for such displays. Are we simply hardwired to bow down to something higher than ourselves? Do we yearn for something to take control of our lives, or we might have to? When I asked Kabir about this, he put forward the case that it's like praying to awaken the Buddha in ourselves, which I found easier to accept. But when talk turned to unseen realms containing gods and goddesses, I felt like I'd wandered into a Hans Christian Andersen tale. And it's depressing to think that even the different strains of Buddhism can be antagonistic towards each other. There's still much I like about the teachings, which I continue to read, but I don't think I'll be shaving my head anytime soon. Which is a shame, because I really have the skull for it.

Regrettably, it was while we were all having lunch with Kabir that a head cold really started to kick in, and I was about to experience my own night of the dark soul. I retired to my room, where it didn't take long for a very bad cold to turn into chronic diarrhoea. My shoulder had been playing up, so I had organised a shiatsu massage for late that afternoon, and I didn't cancel, thinking that any distraction from my can would be welcome. He was a lovely man who worked as a waiter in two restaurants as well as being a masseur. At the end, he said that if I helped him come to Australia he would massage my family every day. Considering my single childless status, that's a pretty cushy job he was angling for. Or maybe he was just angling for the tip I gave him, because I'm sure he was as aware as I was that that was all I could really do. The massage took place with me fully clothed on the bed, and at one point he lay completely on top of me. I don't know what was more disconcerting, having a man lie on top of me for the first time in a while, or being aware of the fact that his weight on my bowel might have meant that I was going to experience a very different release from the one I'd been hoping for.

The next day we travelled to Varanasi, one of the oldest continually occupied cities, along with Jerusalem, in the world. It is the Hindu god and yogi Shiva's city, a holy city where it is propitious to die, and this would be the place that really affected me on our trip.

I found Varanasi quite overwhelming, with life and death being thrown in your face. This is where the funeral ghats, or steps, meet the Ganges, and burning bodies are pushed out into the river. We saw three services taking place one night and it was like something from another time. It was a long way from the cold room where I saw my parents' coffins disappear into the floor to be cremated. But there was so much life in Varanasi, too. Pigs and cows are everywhere, and everything seemed to happen in the street, from pissing to haircuts.

We interviewed an American woman called Shavani (she was christened Vera Lee), who ran a café, which was no mean feat for a 63-year-old single lady in this town. To be honest, initially I thought that she was a little unhinged. She moved to India because she was a Shiva devotee, and it was important for her to live near the Ganges. She seemed to be constantly on the verge of tears and I wondered if she just needed a good lie down, and also if she'd be better off back in the States whiling away the hours watching *Jeopardy!* But I was blown away by her passion and the courage of her decision to so radically change her life after being a wife and mother back home. Her basic belief is that we're here to know ourselves and help others, and I found much about her inspiring. She also gave me a big, fat wake-up call: she told me I was very lucky to be going on this journey, to have this opportunity, which is something I felt daily. Then she said, 'Do you have kids?' Of course, I said I didn't. Then she asked if I had a partner and when I again replied in the negative, she said, 'You're so lucky! You're so free! You can do whatever you want.'

I know that this is bone-crushingly obvious, but sometimes it takes a total stranger to snap you out of your own bullshit. While logically I knew how fortunate I was, and that a man was certainly not the answer, I somehow needed to hear it from someone else, someone who'd had to wait years to follow her passion because of a man and family commitments. Oh God, don't tell me that I had to go on a journey to find . . . myself? But what did I expect? I was going to go on a voyage of self-discovery and find one of the Affleck brothers?

That night we attended a puja, or ceremony, by the banks of the Ganges, which was dedicated to the great life-giving river. It was incredible. Seven young priests conducted it, and their synchronised movements and chanting were mesmerising (not to mention a little like the Backstreet Boys). We interviewed a much older priest beforehand who told me that it doesn't matter if you aren't Hindu, all you have to do is open your heart while the puja is taking place and you'll find peace. He had a flair for the dramatic, but he also assured me that I would be affected because Mother Ganga had called me. This may well be a speech he gives to every tourist, but it turned out to be true.

We filmed it all and, for a very minimal fee, I was involved in the proceedings. They gave me a blessing before the main part of the ceremony, which involved me throwing various flowers and plates of rice and other offerings into the river. Surrounded by these young men, on the banks of the Ganges on a perfect night, it did feel like I was involved in something sacred. I knew that many of the people watching me from the crowd that gathers nightly would have viewed me as extremely lucky, and that's how I felt.

I should add that I was still pretty sick, so I was Codralled out of my mind. This may have had something to do with how emotional I felt, but I found this particular evening one of the most special on the journey. Despite the fact that money had changed hands, I was overwhelmed by the generosity of the people who included me in the service. That, combined with being involved in something so ancient, was simply overwhelming. It was hard not to be aware of how insignificant and impermanent we are compared to something like this great river. Tragically, the point was reinforced only months after we returned home, when a bomb exploded, killing several people in the very place where we'd been that night.

The next day began with a dawn trip up the Ganges. I know that the river is meant to be much polluted, but it was still extraordinary, as was seeing the life it supports: people bathing, washing their clothes and, sure, probably defecating. Someone pointed out to me that people do think of the river as a mother, and that we don't always treat our mothers well.

I was yet to do some yoga and for some reason this was the one request the super-efficient Deepak and his assistant, Rinchin, were not on top of, and it was only organised at the last minute. Ironically, yoga is now only gaining popularity in India again because of how many people have embraced it in the West. The country is full of charlatans in this field – preying on fools like me who want some sort of ultimate yoga experience. Deepak knew nothing about yoga, but he assured me that the teacher they'd found was the real deal.

When we arrived, a young man was waiting with an older one who certainly looked like a yogi – well, he actually looked like a ratty Osho (the Orange People guy), but it didn't matter because he was just along for the ride and we never found out who the hell he was. Ram, the younger gentleman, was the teacher. While I knew that it would look beautiful for the camera, my first concern was when I realised that we were going to conduct the class on the uneven roof of a boat on the Ganges. This made about as much sense as wrestling in jelly . . . hang on a minute . . .

It then didn't take long for me to work out that I know more about yoga than Ram does. At one point he said, 'You have an excellent practice,' and I thought, 'A mushroom would have a better grip on this.' He just seemed bored. He'd get me to do a pose on one side of the body and not bother doing the other, and at one point I opened my eyes to see him checking his phone messages. This was towards the end of our trip, and I have to admit that 'incredible India' was starting to look a little less incredible. What was I really expecting? Did I think one yoga class with an Indian teacher would change my life?

The trip back on the river at dusk was as beautiful as the morning journey, but I was tired and pissed off that I could have had a better yoga experience in a gym in Australia. When an enormous cockroach ran up my arm as I made to eat another mouthful of chips from a packet, I started to think, 'Incredible India, my arse.' I was sick of people demanding money from me, whether it was hotel staff or anyone in the street, I never wanted to eat another curry again as long as I lived, and I wanted to use a proper fucking toilet. I wanted to go home.

The next day, I took part in another puja on the river that was about my ancestors. I dedicated it to Mum and Dad. It was a scorching day and we were besieged with beggars. The ceremony involved me reciting Sanskrit for about forty-five minutes and I felt like I was hanging on by a thread. I butchered the language to such an extent that our director Brendan thought I was actually saying, 'Ita Buttrose, Ita Buttrose,' over and over again. This was nothing like the moving experience from the other evening, especially when the person conducting it took a phone call from what I decided was his bookie.

The same priest had organised this puja and seemed to want more money than had been previously agreed. I found his grand statements a lot less impressive this time round. When his final words to me were, 'You will come back to Varanasi again and again and again,' I remember thinking that I'm more likely to be impregnated by Ronald Reagan.

The last day, we did pick-up shots in Delhi. At one point, a little girl approached Jo and I, and we were both thinking the same thing – she wanted money. But she didn't. She just wanted to shake our hands and give us a flower and a huge smile. It was starting to look like the self that I'd 'found' in India was just a bit of a bitch.

On the verge of leaving, though, I didn't want to go. Looking back over my diary entries, they are both extreme and deeply embarrassing. Ten days is such a short time, but I definitely went on a journey. It was Kabir who had said, 'Who knows how all this will affect you down the track? Who knows what seeds have been planted?'

Who does know? I'm sure I will return. We seem so sanitised in the West. I can't believe I worried about a cockroach. The impermanence of life isn't hidden in India. Shavani said that she was shocked one day when she saw a dog walk by with a dead baby in its mouth, but then thought, 'Well, that's what happens.' Sometimes, it was hard to reconcile something like that with constantly pulling out hand disinfectant every time you touched something. What were we really trying to protect ourselves from?

Buddhist nun Robina Courtin said that the act of search-ing was something in itself, and I understand why people go to India to do it. It's so different for those of us from the West, that the shift can't help but make you question how you live your life and what's important. And the spiritual is everywhere. I think that's what moved me about Varanasi, in particular. In Bodh Gaya, Buddhism felt more contained, it revolved around the temples, whereas the life in and around the Ganges is all about Shiva and Hinduism. And the same people who worship are the ones that sit on the banks with magnets attached to strings to attract the jewellery from the bodies that have been farewelled into the river: the sacred and the profane.

Our fixer Deepak was more than forthcoming about his beliefs. He told me matter-of-factly about a vision he'd had of Shiva in a cave, and how he'd actually 'felt' Shiva's locks of hair hit him in the face. He also spoke of how he and his sister saw and photographed a monkey god that is meant to be one of the few deities still living among us. He told me this like he was talking about thinking of growing a beard. Part of me found these stories just astonishing but, again, his belief was undenia-ble. I have no idea what he and his sister did see, but Deepak is a kind man, full of intelligence and compassion, and if this is part of the story that gives his life meaning, who am I to argue? All I know is that he was part of the kindest incident that I witnessed while making the television series.

It was impossible not to feel white guilt while we were in India, and the Australians all talked about it. Can you imagine how difficult their poverty was on *us*? We were doing it so tough . . . Finally, Deepak said that he couldn't afford to give everyone money either, but that he tried to live as Gandhi suggested. The quote was something along the lines of: 'I judge a man by how he treats the poorest of the poor.' Two nights after that, when we were in Varanasi, a young boy approached us selling postcards. There were so many things wrong with him that it was difficult to even look at him. Deepak simply walked up to this kid, put his arm around his shoulders and then walked with him for five minutes, talking and laughing. I don't know that anything moved me as much as that moment. I remember thinking, 'Who is this guy? Jesus?' and 'Please sleep with me.'

While I completely understand the lure of India, or any kind of travel, to instigate change in a person's life, it's obviously the desire for change that's the catalyst, and that means it could also happen at your local mall or in your toilet. Certainly, some of the most wonderful moments I had during the series were in my own country, but I was grateful for all of it.

Obviously, India and my experience with the Aboriginal elders had been amazing, and the series confirmed my interest in both yoga and meditation, but more than anything, it made me more tolerant of other people's beliefs. As long as you're not hurting anyone or judging others, then knock yourself out. It also made me realise that the people I admire the most are the ones who are still questioning. Some of these people are aligned with a certain faith and some of them aren't, but they all have a curiosity and an openness about them. I honestly think that the only people who are really nuts are the ones who think they know the answer. God knows, it took me years to work out that there was even a question.

12

BRISVEGAS

Meditation is now a constant part of my life. It has made a big difference, but it's not easy. I think a lot of people think that if you meditate regularly you'll turn into a beacon of calm and peace – that's certainly what I used to think. Maybe you do eventually, but I haven't found this to be the case. It's really difficult. The mind never stops producing thoughts but during meditation you try to not attach to them. You acknowledge them and then return to your breathing (at least, that's the technique I use). It makes you much more aware of your internal dialogue and the patterns of your own mind. The whole process can bring up a lot of stuff; it can make you angry or depressed. A friend of mine told me she had to stop for a while because she started seeing a terrifying monster when she tried to enter a relaxed state. I'm not meaning to make it sound like the movie *Requiem for a Dream*. I also enjoy moments of tranquillity and stillness. It never lasts for long, but to experience the quiet when there is a tiny break in your thoughts, even for a couple of seconds, is a wonderful feeling. Your mind is still and you feel present, a part of being here, as opposed to worrying about bills, work or why you ate that packet of beef jerky for lunch.

I'm really on the bottom rung of the ladder when it comes to stilling the mind, so I'm not speaking with any great authority. But I'm guessing that the more you do it, the more you have these moments of 'dazzling darkness', as I heard one person describe it. And I'm sure that, in turn, this probably leads to some amazing experiences, but I believe the aim is to accept whatever is happening, rather than to evaluate whether it's 'good' or 'bad'. No doubt even the Dalai Lama has fleeting moments, like 'Did I lock the front door of the temple? I really need to take a crap, and man, that guy sitting next to me is just a prick.'

Before the TV series, the only time that I'd really meditated regularly was about three years ago, when I was on tour, because I'd clicked that it seemed to help a bit with my stress levels and made me feel less like I was turning into a squirrel. Towards the end of the run of shows, I spent three weeks in Brisbane and had a couple of spooky experiences. As well as meditating, I was trying consciously to do the whole 'being present' thing and one morning something pretty incredible happened.

I was eating fruit salad for breakfast and found myself looking at a passionfruit, but I mean, REALLY looking at it, in a way that I felt I never had before. I wasn't thinking about the show or anything else. I was completely *there* and it was incredible. This goddamn passionfruit was the most beautiful thing I'd ever seen. I was filled with euphoria and started laughing like a crazy person, because I finally understood how wonderful being truly in the moment could be. Yes, I know. If you think that it sounds like I was just having a psychotic episode, don't read the next paragraph.

I really considered not putting this in the book. I haven't told most of my friends this story because they'll think I had a breakdown or an acid trip. Make up your own mind.

The day after the passionfruit experience, I was walking through the botanical gardens and it happened again, except this time it probably lasted for about two hours. I was completely there. It felt like my senses were all on overdrive – I could feel every little breeze, hear every tiny noise and I was simply drunk on what my eyes were seeing. Every plant or flower, every ray of light that bounced off a surface was just amazing. I felt like I was moving in slow motion. At one point, I passed through a street market and felt completely connected to every person there. Some classical music was playing and it felt like everyone was engaged in some giant choreographed number, where we were all doing exactly what we were meant to be doing. That feeling continued when I saw people walking in the park and when I picked up a ball to hand it back to a father who was playing with his little girl. Everything felt exactly right. We were all part of something much larger, and it was perfect. I've never felt such a feeling of wellbeing. I've never felt such pure happiness. It did feel like a drug, and towards the end of it, I panicked.

I was losing the sense of being present, as my mind wasn't coping with what was happening. It was so different from anything that I'd felt before and I think I worried that if it didn't end, I would somehow not get back to my old life. It's nuts, but it was like I thought I'd be locked in the Narnia wardrobe forever. I haven't experienced anything like it since and I still can't really explain it. Okay, now someone can call an ambulance.

As mystical 'I'm one with the universe' experiences go, this is as good as it's ever gotten for me. Yet I was half-hearted about wanting that feeling again. The more time has passed, the more I marvel at how little I thought about those couple of hours or desired their return. It really was a kind of bliss, but I didn't want to go back there.

The truth is, I think, that it really did scare me. I lost all sense of 'me' and my mind isn't used to that. What would 'I' do without the ceaseless jabbering in my head, the constant fantasising, worrying about the future, regretting the past, replaying conversations again and again? 'I' would disappear, in some sense, and whatever was left would feel connected with everything around and at some sort of peace – WHO WANTS THAT?

I don't think what I felt was *that* unusual, either – at least I didn't tell you about the time I thought I was Zeus. I think most of us have had that feeling of being truly in the moment and forgetting ourselves, whether it was when giving birth, performing, doing something creative or even being in a life-threatening situation. Time is immaterial and so are we.

The only time I've been back to Queensland since then was to visit Peter Kennedy for *Spiritual Journey*. He's the rebel priest who bent the rules and questioned some basic tenets of Catholicism and hence was thrown out of his parish. He now conducts his services in a room in the Trades and Labor Council building in Brisbane. Peter had turned his old parish into a very popular one and a lot of his congregation has followed him.

There was much about his service I liked: the welcome to country, the number of women involved and even the fact that 'the homily' was a piece about Mental Health Week. Predictably, I had problems with the familiar stuff: the Our Father, the prayers of the faithful and, the guts of the mass, the Eucharist.

I wondered how I could avoid the Body of Christ as various people came around with pieces of bread, but then a woman, Clare, walked up and said, 'We're all worthy here.' So I had it; I felt it would be rude not to. Later, she told me that one of the aspects she loves about this community is that she never feels judged, and I had to admit I was touched by her gesture of inclusion. Generally, I enjoyed myself, because people were friendly, open and genuinely seemed to want to be there, and I was impressed that the newsletter referred to the fact that they were close to achieving their goal of helping the fifty worst-off homeless people in Brisbane. And when a woman told me that I'd lost some weight, I knew that this was the place for me, because the most important part of a spiritual life, to my mind, is feeling trim.

I loved Peter. It turned out that the elements of the 'mass' I felt uncomfortable with are the ones he wants to lose. He doesn't believe in prayer, Communion, the Virgin Birth . . . he's a little like Marlon Brando in *The Wild One* – whatever the Church has 'got' he's happy to rebel against, or at least question. Here is another person that has been searching all his life, and who, now in his seventies, no longer calls himself a priest or a Catholic. He's scathing of the institution but acknowledges people's need for community and spirituality. He has very much embraced Eastern philosophy and has far more time for author Eckhart Tolle than he does for the Pope. I can honestly say that if I lived in the same city as him, I think I would join his flock.

And it was back to Peter's flock that I returned at the end of the TV series, to give a homily summing up my experiences – tough gig. I talked about my Catholic upbringing, walking away from the Church, and my years of atheism and booze. How I'd looked for meaning in my career and relationships and yet it wasn't until my parents died that I really started to question everything. Yoga started me on this 'journey' that led to this book and the series, in which I wanted to talk about spirituality with some humour and hopefully without disappearing up my own lower intestine. It helped open me up. It stopped me from being so dismissive of everything, because that approach to living had gotten me nowhere. It helped me understand, along with meditation, that discovering how your mind works so that you can befriend it is one of the most useful things you can do. And it also helped me realise that trying to live in this very moment really makes sense, even though it's deceptively difficult and a little scary, because it does involve a lack of control. But then, I don't think we have that much control anyway.

But while yoga and meditation have certainly worked for me, it became very clear while making the show that different things obviously work for different people, and I no longer feel in a position to write off any method, and that includes atheism. I was particularly struck by this when we interviewed the performer Philip Escoffey for the series. Philip is content with the awesomeness of the universe and doesn't need any kind of spirituality in his life. (He paraphrased Douglas Adams: 'There's enough wonder in the garden without fairies at the bottom of it.') I agree with pretty much everything he says and, to be honest, I'm still only a degree or two off being an atheist myself, although sometimes I wonder how much of it gets down to semantics. I've spoken to many atheists who don't believe in religion or any kind of belief system, but they do believe in love or art or, like Philip, simply have a sense of wonder about the universe – some people would call that God.

And would probably say that's what I experienced at certain times throughout the show, such as when I was moved by a Hindu ceremony on the Ganges, because I was included in the same way that I was by Sisters Rebecca, Margaret and Pauline, and by the people of Peter Kennedy's church. I was also impressed by the desire of all these people to help others. And

I was equally affected by feeling so small and yet connected to something larger, both in Varanasi and in the desert outside of Alice Springs.

I am so incredibly grateful to all the people we met who shared so much of themselves, and I miss them. I miss getting up every day and thinking of nothing but this wonderful question of life.

I have no doubt that I have many hangovers and bad decisions still ahead of me, but I do want to appreciate any time I have left. I try to be all 'Power of Now' when I can, and to remember that I'm just an infinitesimal part of something huge and often downright ridiculous (I mean, Shane Warne and Elizabeth Hurley are together, for God's sake). I also don't doubt that my ideas about the point of life will keep shifting, and I should hope so too. The last book I read, given to me by the wonderful Peter Kennedy, suggests that not only are we all connected, but that *everything* is God – we're all part of one consciousness. So while everything matters, in a way, also, nothing does, because nothing is ever really lost. I don't know if that's true but I like the idea. I like the idea that Olivia, Lynda, my parents and everyone we lose have simply returned to what we all return to, and that somehow they have played a part in a plan so vast it is simply beyond our comprehension.

Life is so wonderful, horrible and crazy, all you can really do is strap yourself in. Somebody turn that into a bumper sticker.

Acknowledgements

Thank you to everyone at Penguin, especially the very lovely and patient Michael Nolan and the quite simply miraculous Ben Ball. Ben almost literally had to pick me up and drag me over the finish line on this one, and if anyone thinks that I can write at all, it is thanks to Mr Ball.

As always I would like to thank everyone at Token Artists, particularly the wonderful Dioni Meliss, Georgina Ogilvie (like I was going to leave you out this time) and the funniest manager in showbiz – and my pal – Kevin Whyte.

Thank you to everyone involved in Judith Lucy's Spiritual Journey: whether you were in front of the camera or behind it, you were all, without exception, top-shelf. I pretty much leapt out of bed every day I worked on the show, and if I could make love to each and every one of you, I would (sorry if that idea is mildly repulsive to some, if not all of you). There are too many to name, so I'm pretty much going to limit it to those who influenced me in terms of the book. A special thank you to Courtney Gibson, who got the ball rolling, and to everyone at the ABC who let me make the damn thing, especially Sophia Zachariou and the terrific Amanda Duthie.

Thank you Todd Abbott, Robyn Smith, Jo Chichester, Andy Walker, Brendan Fletcher, Frank Bruzzese, Chris Branagan, Barry Nichols, Tony

Martin, Rinchin Yolmo and Deepak Chaturvedi.

Thank you also Brett Kirk, Peter Kennedy, Fr Gerald Gleeson, Frank Woodley, Jungala Kriss, Gloria McCormack, Maggie Cowins, Beryl Collins, Lily Bragge, Mark Yettica-Paulson, Sr Rebecca McCabe, Robina Courtin, Allan Panozza, Philip Escoffey and Greg Fleet.

Thank you to all my friends and family. A special thanks, for their advice and support with the book, to Lady Chooky Cripps (some know her as Kaz Cooke) and the viper himself, Colin Batrouney.

Thank you to Al Mullins, Gareth Skinner, Collin Scott, Michelle Hovane, Denise Scott and Louise Goodvach, for reading certain parts of the book early and not throwing up.

And finally, whether you're in the book or not (and most of you are), thank you for being part of the journey, man: Andrea Powell, Ann, Michael and Mark Hovane, Jayne Dullard, Helen Anderson, Robyn Byron, Andrew Creagh, Gillian Lemon, Steve Briggs, Craig Fitzgerald, Lynda Gibson, Warwick Hunter, Sue Bignell, Amanda Blair, Annie Maver, David Pottinger, Jan Healey, Ann, Tony and Niall Lucy, Elizabeth Millet, Emma Moss, Peter Helliar, Sal Upton, Mick, Richard and John Molloy, Pip Brennan and Audrey Fairthorne.